Building Android UIs with Custom Views

Build amazing custom user interfaces with Android custom views

Raimon Ràfols Montané

BIRMINGHAM - MUMBAI

Building Android UIs with Custom Views

First published: October 2017

Production reference: 1241017

Published by Packt Publishing Ltd.
Livery Place
35 Livery Street
Birmingham
B3 2PB, UK.

ISBN 978-1-78588-286-9

www.packtpub.com

Credits

Author
Raimon Ràfols Montané

Reviewer
Basil Miller

Commissioning Editor
Amarabha Banerjee

Acquisition Editor
Reshma Raman

Content Development Editor
Sreeja Nair

Technical Editor
Leena Patil

Copy Editor
Safis Editing

Project Coordinator
Sheejal Shah

Proofreader
Safis Editing

Indexer
Rekha Nair

Graphics
Jason Monteiro

Production Coordinator
Melwyn D'sa

About the Author

Raimon Ràfols Montané is a software engineer currently living in the Barcelona area. He has been working on mobile devices since their early stages, ranging from monochrome devices to the current smartphones. During this time, he has worked in several areas: B2C/B2E/B2B apps, portals, and mobile gaming. Due to this broad experience, he has expertise in many technologies and, especially in UI, build systems, and client-server communications.

He is currently working as an engineering manager at AXA Group Solutions in Barcelona, taking care of all the engineering and development processes, mobile application quality, and leading the R&D team. In the past, he has worked abroad for Imagination Technologies near London and for Service2Media in the Netherlands.

In his spare time, he enjoys taking part in hackathons, photography, and speaking at conferences. Raimon has won more than 40 international awards, including AngelHack Barcelona 2015, Facebook World Hack Barcelona. Also, he has secured the second place at JS1k 2016. He was the chairman of the Transforming Industries Summit at the Mobile World Congress Shanghai 2017, where he also spoke about Enterprise Transformation. In addition, he has given talks speaking about Android and Java performance, bytecode, custom views, and entrepreneurship in at several conferences around the world.

In addition, Raimon is the coauthor of Learning *Android Application Development*, also published by Packt, and he has been the technical reviewer of several other titles, including *Mastering Android NDK* and *Android Things Projects*, among others.

Acknowledgements

I'd really like to thank Laia Gomà; without your love, patience, and understanding, this book wouldn't have been possible. Also, I'd like to thank Rafa Cosin and my parents, as without their support and encouragement, I'd not be doing what I do today.

I'd also like to thank everyone who inspired my curiosity about real-time computer graphics and performance. Without that inspiration, I wouldn't have started building custom views and I definitely wouldn't be speaking at conferences about low-level bytecode.

Last but not least, I'd like to thank everyone who challenged me and helped me grow in my professional career; people like Enric Agut, Diego Morales, Alfred Ferrer, Carlos Carrasco, Pau Vivancos, Miquel Barceló, David Domingo, Marcel Roorda, Alberto Chamorro, Teun van Run, Tom van Wietmarschen, Josep Cedó, Yves Caseau, Joanne Pupo, Jordi Valldaura, Mathieu Sivade, Chris Jakob, Tomas Kustrzynski, Ramon Salla, Bartłomiej Zarnowski, Radosław Holewa, Inigo Quilez, and all those who I have forgotten to mention here.

About the Reviewer

Basil Miller is the cofounder of Devlight. An Ivano-Frankivsk based leading Android developer, Basil has over 4 years' experience of being a developer, which has endowed him with the opportunity to hold his current position.

His educational background includes a bachelor's degree in computer science, which he enhanced by attending Java SE courses for 1 year. Besides the status of cofounder, organizer, and speaker of GDG Ivano-Frankivsk, Basil is a part of the core team of Devlight. This technical background has enabled him to develop and train some personal skills, such as team organizing, self-employment, and communication.

Since 2014, Android developers all over the world have been watching his progress and using his free products developed in the role of open source Android UI widgets provider. His products are focused on project architecture, adhering to guidelines, code glance, long-lasting integration, and much more. Another significant achievement are his third-party libraries, which have reached the top of the popular trend charts and stayed there for a long time.

During his time working as a part of Devlight, a lot of products for business solutions were projected and organized by Basil. Projects that he usually works on relate to fintech, currency exchange, delivery services, social networks, and payment system SDKs. His personal duties on the afore mentioned projects are UI implementation, structure creation, team leading, and technical support. Therefore, he has gained the following key skills and competencies: a master's degree in UI realization (canvas, animations, and layout framework), mentoring new developers, and strong knowledge of custom views.

Being a cofounder of Devlight, Basil is able and willing to collaborate on work on the new business projects and start-ups. Also, it is easy to contact Basil in order to involve him into projects as a mobile development consultant.

Basil has garnered recognition among coworkers, partners, and developers abroad. So, the business of Devlight and its achievements are associated with the name Basil Miller.

www.PacktPub.com

For support files and downloads related to your book, please visit www.PacktPub.com.

Did you know that Packt offers eBook versions of every book published, with PDF and ePub files available? You can upgrade to the eBook version at www.PacktPub.com and as a print book customer, you are entitled to a discount on the eBook copy. Get in touch with us at service@packtpub.com for more details.

At www.PacktPub.com, you can also read a collection of free technical articles, sign up for a range of free newsletters and receive exclusive discounts and offers on Packt books and eBooks.

https://www.packtpub.com/mapt

Get the most in-demand software skills with Mapt. Mapt gives you full access to all Packt books and video courses, as well as industry-leading tools to help you plan your personal development and advance your career.

Why subscribe?

- Fully searchable across every book published by Packt
- Copy and paste, print, and bookmark content
- On demand and accessible via a web browser

Customer Feedback

Thanks for purchasing this Packt book. At Packt, quality is at the heart of our editorial process. To help us improve, please leave us an honest review on this book's Amazon page at `https://www.amazon.com/dp/1785882864`.

If you'd like to join our team of regular reviewers, you can e-mail us at `customerreviews@packtpub.com`. We award our regular reviewers with free eBooks and videos in exchange for their valuable feedback. Help us be relentless in improving our products!

Table of Contents

Preface

Many years ago, before the launch of Android and the iPhone, one of the major concerns was having a central place to purchase and download mobile applications. Nowadays, we manage to solve this issue with widely available centralized application stores such as Google Play, at the expense of application discoverability.

Google Play, like any other mobile application store, is highly saturated. Unless an application does something unique or has something special, it's extremely hard to stand out from the dozens of applications doing approximately the same, or even if they're completely unrelated.

Increasing marketing spending might temporarily alleviate the issue but, in the long term, applications still need to figure out that unique functionality or that detail that makes them different.

One way to make a distinctive application is to slightly diverge from the Android standard widgets and UI components and include a specific custom view custom menu, or, at the end of the day, anything that makes it exceptional. We should be aware that this doesn't mean we should completely ignore the Android standard widgets and rewrite the whole UI of the application. As with almost everything, do user tests and discover what works and what doesn't work for them. Explore new options and solve the pains they have, but don't overdo it. Sometimes, creating a particular menu on top of your application might solve navigation problems, or a well-defined animation might communicate the right transition for the application's users.

In this book, we will see how to start building custom views for Android and integrate them into our applications. We'll see in detail how to interact with them and add animations and comprehensive examples, both using 2D and 3D rendering capabilities. Finally, we will also see how to share our custom views so they can be reused in our enterprise environment, and also how to open source them and make them available to the Android development community.

What this book covers

Chapter 1, *Getting Started*, explains what custom views are and when we need them, and shows you how to build your first custom view.

Chapter 2, *Implementing Your First Custom View*, covers in more details about measurement, instantiating, parameterizing, and some basic rendering to start getting a feeling for what we can do with custom views.

Chapter 3, *Handling Events*, shows the reader how to make a custom view interactive and react to user interactions.

Chapter 4, *Advanced 2D Rendering*, adds additional rendering primitives and operations and how to combine them to build more complex custom views.

Chapter 5, *Introducing 3D Custom Views*, as we are not only limited to 2D rendering, this chapter introduces how we can use OpenGL ES to render custom Views in 3D.

Chapter 6, *Animations*, covers how to add animations to custom views, both by using standard Android components and by doing it ourselves.

Chapter 7, *Performance Considerations*, exposes some recommendations and best practices when building a custom view and what the impact of not following them could be.

Chapter 8, *Sharing Our Custom View*, covers how to package and share our custom view and make it publicly available.

Chapter 9, *Implementing Your Own EPG*, shows how to build a more complex example of a custom view by combining many of the things we've seen in the book.

Chapter 10, *Building a Charts Component*, shows in detail how to build a chart custom view and make it customizable step by step.

Chapter 11, *Creating a 3D Spinning Wheel Menu*, covers how to build a more complex 3D custom view that can be used as a selection menu.

What you need for this book

In order to follow the examples in this book, you'll need Android Studio installed. We'll briefly cover how to install and set up a device emulator in the first chapter. It's highly recommended to get at least Android Studio 3.0. At the time of writing this book, Android Studio 3.0 is still beta, but stable enough to develop, run, and test all the examples. In addition, our recommendation is to have an Android device to better experience user interactions in the custom views we'll create, but they will also work in an Android emulator.

Who this book is for

This book is for developers who want to improve their Android application development skills and build an Android application using custom views.

Conventions

In this book, you will find a number of text styles that distinguish between different kinds of information. Here are some examples of these styles and an explanation of their meaning.

Code words in text, database table names, folder names, filenames, file extensions, pathnames, dummy URLs, user input, and Twitter handles are shown as follows:

"We can use the getWidth() and getHeight() methods to get the width and height, respectively, of the view."

A block of code is set as follows:

```
<com.packt.rrafols.customview.OwnTextView
        android:layout_width="wrap_content"
        android:layout_height="wrap_content"
        android:text="Hello World!" />
```

When we wish to draw your attention to a particular part of a code block, the relevant lines or items are set in bold:

```
float maxLabelWidth = 0.f;
if (regenerate) {
    for (int i = 0; i<= 10; i++) {
        float step;
  if (!invertVerticalAxis) {
    step = ((float) i / 10.f);
```

```
  } else {
    step = ((float) (10 - i)) / 10.f;
  }
```

New terms and important words are shown in bold, for example, they appear in the text like this: "The layouts are usually known as **ViewGroup.**"

 Warnings or important notes appear in a box like this.

 Tips and tricks appear like this.

Reader feedback

Feedback from our readers is always welcome. Let us know what you think about this book-what you liked or disliked. Reader feedback is important for us as it helps us develop titles that you will really get the most out of.

To send us general feedback, simply e-mail feedback@packtpub.com, and mention the book's title in the subject of your message.

If there is a topic that you have expertise in and you are interested in either writing or contributing to a book, see our author guide at www.packtpub.com/authors.

Customer support

Now that you are the proud owner of a Packt book, we have a number of things to help you to get the most from your purchase.

Downloading the example code

You can download the example code files for this book from your account at http://www.packtpub.com. If you purchased this book elsewhere, you can visit http://www.packtpub.com/support and register to have the files e-mailed directly to you.

You can download the code files by following these steps:

1. Log in or register to our website using your e-mail address and password.
2. Hover the mouse pointer on the **SUPPORT** tab at the top.
3. Click on **Code Downloads & Errata**.
4. Enter the name of the book in the **Search** box.
5. Select the book for which you're looking to download the code files.
6. Choose from the drop-down menu where you purchased this book from.
7. Click on **Code Download**.

Once the file is downloaded, please make sure that you unzip or extract the folder using the latest version of:

- WinRAR / 7-Zip for Windows
- Zipeg / iZip / UnRarX for Mac
- 7-Zip / PeaZip for Linux

The code bundle for the book is also hosted on GitHub at `https://github.com/PacktPublishing/Building-Android-UIs-with-Custom-Views`. We also have other code bundles from our rich catalog of books and videos available at `https://github.com/PacktPublishing/`. Check them out!

Errata

Although we have taken every care to ensure the accuracy of our content, mistakes do happen. If you find a mistake in one of our books-maybe a mistake in the text or the code-we would be grateful if you could report this to us. By doing so, you can save other readers from frustration and help us improve subsequent versions of this book. If you find any errata, please report them by visiting `http://www.packtpub.com/submit-errata`, selecting your book, clicking on the **Errata Submission Form** link, and entering the details of your errata. Once your errata are verified, your submission will be accepted and the errata will be uploaded to our website or added to any list of existing errata under the Errata section of that title.

To view the previously submitted errata, go to `https://www.packtpub.com/books/content/support` and enter the name of the book in the search field. The required information will appear under the **Errata** section.

Piracy

Piracy of copyrighted material on the Internet is an ongoing problem across all media. At Packt, we take the protection of our copyright and licenses very seriously. If you come across any illegal copies of our works in any form on the Internet, please provide us with the location address or website name immediately so that we can pursue a remedy.

Please contact us at `copyright@packtpub.com` with a link to the suspected pirated material.

We appreciate your help in protecting our authors and our ability to bring you valuable content.

Questions

If you have a problem with any aspect of this book, you can contact us at `questions@packtpub.com`, and we will do our best to address the problem.

1
Getting Started

You might be wondering what a custom view is; that's alright, we'll cover that and way more in this book. If you've been developing **Android** applications for a while, you've most probably used the standard Android views or widgets tons of times. These are, for example: **TextView**, **ImageView**, **Button**, **ListView**, and so on. A custom view is slightly different. To summarize it quickly, a custom view is a view or a **widget** where we've implemented its behavior ourselves. In this chapter, we'll cover the very basics steps we'll need to get ourselves started building Android custom views and understand where we should use them and where we should simply rely on the Android standard widgets. More specifically, we will talk about the following topics:

- What's a custom view and why do we need them?
- How to set up and configure our environment to develop custom views
- Creating our very own first custom view

What's a custom view

As we have just mentioned, a custom view is a view where we've implemented its behavior ourselves. That was an oversimplification, but it was a good way to start. We don't really have to implement its complete behavior ourselves. Sometimes, it can just be a simple detail, or a more complex feature or even the whole functionality and behavior such as interaction, drawing, resizing, and so on. For example, tweaking the background color of a button as a custom view implementation, it's a simple change, but creating a bitmap-based menu that rotates in 3D is a complete different story in development time and complexity. We'll show how to build both of them in this book but, in this chapter, we'll only focus on the very simple example and we'll add more features in the chapters to come.

Throughout the book, we'll be referring both to custom view and to custom layouts. The same definition of custom view can also be applied to layouts, but with the main difference that a custom layout will help us to lay out the items it contains with the logic we create and position them the precise way we would like. Stay tuned, as later on we'll learn how to do so as well!

The layouts are usually known as **ViewGroup**. The most typical examples and those you probably have heard of and most probably in your applications are: **LinearLayout**, **RelativeLayout**, and **ConstraintLayout**.

To get more information about Android views and Android layouts, we can always refer to the official Android developer documentation:
`https://developer.android.com/develop/index.html`.

The need for custom views

There are lovely Android applications on Google Play and in other markets: *Amazon*, built only using the standard **Android UI widgets** and layouts. There are also many other applications that have that small additional feature that makes our interaction with them easier or simply more pleasing. There is no magic formula, but maybe by just adding something different, something that the user feels like "hey it's not just another app for..." might increase our user retention. It might not be the deal breaker, but it can definitely make the difference sometimes.

Some custom views can cause so much impact that can cause other applications wanting to imitate it or to build something similar. This effect produces a viral marketing of the application and it also gets the developer community involved as many similar components might appear in the form of tutorials or open source libraries. Obviously, this effect only lasts a limited period of time, but if that happens it's definitely worth it for your application as it'll get more popular and well-known between developers because it'll be something special, not just another Android application.

One of the main reasons to create our own custom views for our mobile application is, precisely, to have something special. It might be a menu, a component, a screen, something that might be really needed or even the main functionality for our application or just as an additional feature.

In addition, by creating our custom view we can actually optimize the performance of our application. We can create a specific way of laying out widgets that otherwise will need many hierarchy layers by just using standard Android layouts or a custom view that simplifies rendering or user interaction.

On the other hand, we can easily fall in the error of trying to custom build everything. Android provides an awesome list of widget and layout components that manages a lot of things for ourselves. If we ignore the basic Android framework and try to build everything by ourselves it would be a lot of work. We would potentially struggle with a lot of issues and errors that the Android OS developers already faced or, at least, very similar ones and, to put it up in one sentence, we would be reinventing the wheel.

Examples on the market

We all probably use great apps that are built only using the standard Android UI widgets and layouts, but there are many others that have some custom views that we don't know or we haven't really noticed. The custom views or layouts can sometimes be very subtle and hard to spot.

We'd not be the first ones to have a custom view or layout in our application. In fact, many popular apps have some custom elements in them. Let's show some examples:

The first example will be the *Etsy* application. The *Etsy* application had a custom layout called **StaggeredGridView**. It was even published as open source in GitHub. It has been deprecated since 2015 in favor of Google's own `StaggeredGridLayoutManager` used together with **RecyclerView**.

You can check it yourself by downloading the *Etsy* application from Google Play, but just to have a quick preview, the following screenshot is actually from the *Etsy* application showing the StaggeredGrid layout:

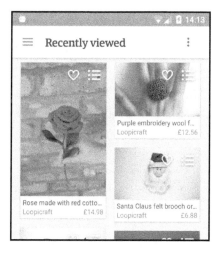

There are many other potential examples, but a second good example might be the electronic programming guide of *Ziggo*, one of the largest cable operators in the Netherlands. The electronic programming guide is a custom view rendering different boxes for the TV shows and changing color for what's ahead and behind current time.

It can be downloaded from the Dutch Google Play only, but anyway, the following screenshot shows how the application is rendering the electronic programming guide:

Finally, a third example and a more recently published application is *Lottie* from Airbnb. *Lottie* is a sample application that renders **Adobe After Effects** animations in real time.

Lottie can be downloaded directly from Google Play, but the following screenshot shows a quick preview of the application:

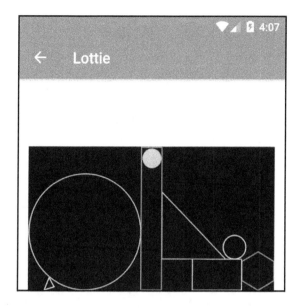

The rendering view and the custom font are examples of custom rendering. For more information about *Lottie* refer to:

`http://airbnb.design/introducing-lottie/.`

We've just seen some examples, but there are many more available. A good site to discover them or to see what is available is Android Arsenal:

`https://android-arsenal.com/.`

Setting up the environment

Now that we have had a brief introduction to custom views, why we need them, and some examples on the market, let's get ourselves started building our own. Our first natural step, if we haven't already done so, is to install Android development tools. If you've got Android Studio already installed, you can skip this section and go directly to the action. Most examples in this book will work perfectly with Android Studio 2.3.3, but later chapters will require Android Studio 3.0. At the time of writing, Android Studio 3.0 is still in beta, but it is highly recommended for testing all the examples provided.

Installing development tools

In order to get started creating your own custom views, you only need what you'll normally need to develop Android mobile applications. In this book, we will be using Android Studio, as it's the tool recommended by Google.

We can get the latest version of Android Studio from its official site:
`https://developer.android.com/studio/index.html`.

Once we've downloaded the package for our computer, we can proceed with the installation:

Now, we can create a new project that we'll use to take our first baby steps on custom views.

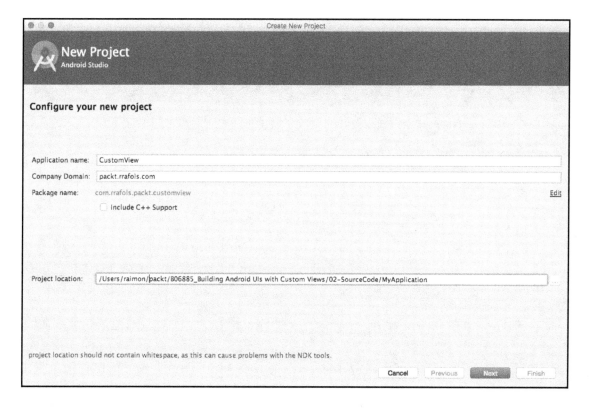

After selecting the **Application name**, the **Company Domain**, which will be reversed into the application **Package name** and the **Project location**, Android Studio will ask us what type of project we want to create:

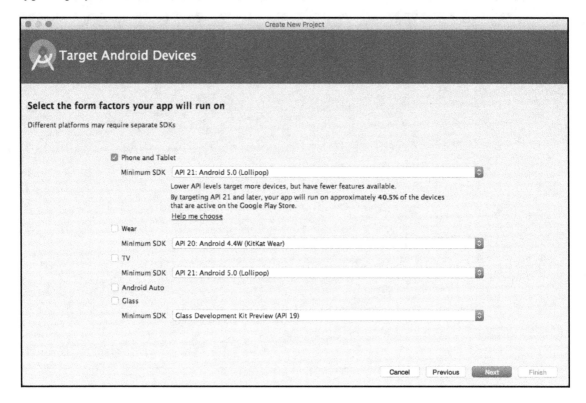

For this example, we don't need anything too fancy, just phone and tablet and API 21 support is more than enough. Once we've done that, we can add an **Empty Activity**:

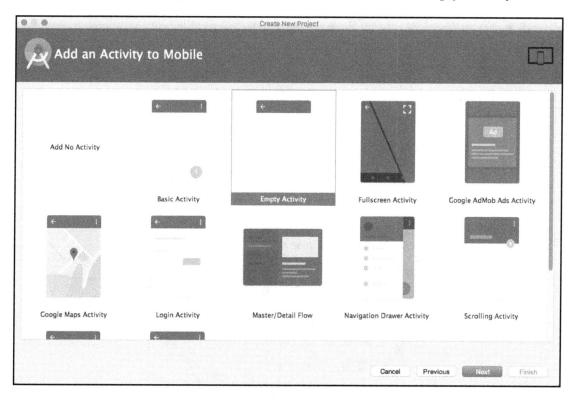

In the case you need help installing Android Studio, there is a step by step guide on the *Learning Android Application Development, Packt Publishing* or there is always plenty of information on the Android developer documentation site. For more information, refer to: `https://www.packtpub.com/application-development/learning-android-application-d evelopment`

Now, we are ready to run this app on a device emulator or on a real device.

How to set up an emulator

To set up an emulator we need to run the **Android Virtual Device Manager (AVD Manager)**. We can find its icon on the top bar, just next to the play/stop application icons.

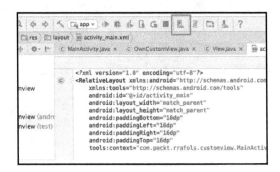

Once we've executed the **Android Device Manager**, we can add or manage our virtual devices from there, as shown in the following screenshot:

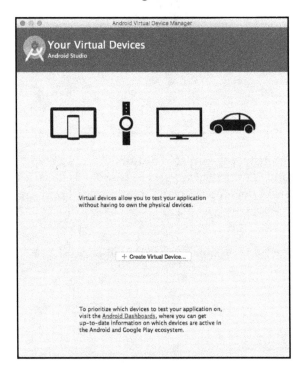

Clicking on **Create Virtual Device** will give us the opportunity to use one of the Android device definitions or even create our own hardware profile, as shown in the following screenshot:

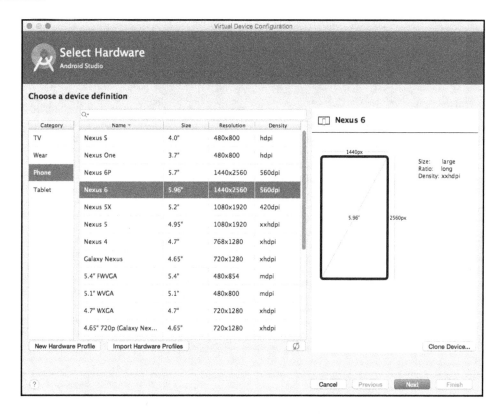

Once we've selected the hardware, we've got to choose the software, or the system image, that will run on it. Later on, we can add all the combinations we need for testing: multiple different devices, or the same device with different Android version images, or even a combination of both.

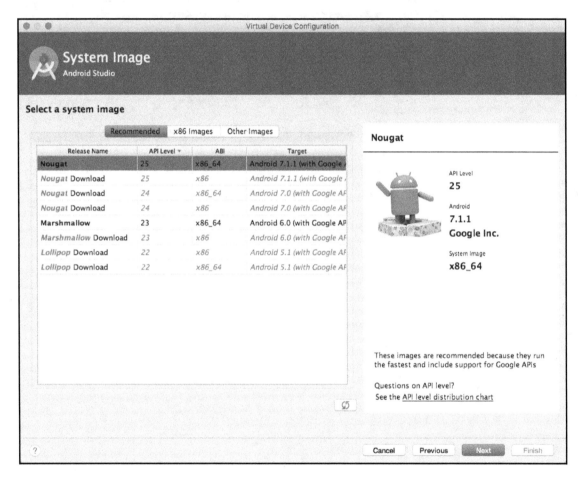

The last step is to name our AVD, review our hardware and software selection, and we're set!

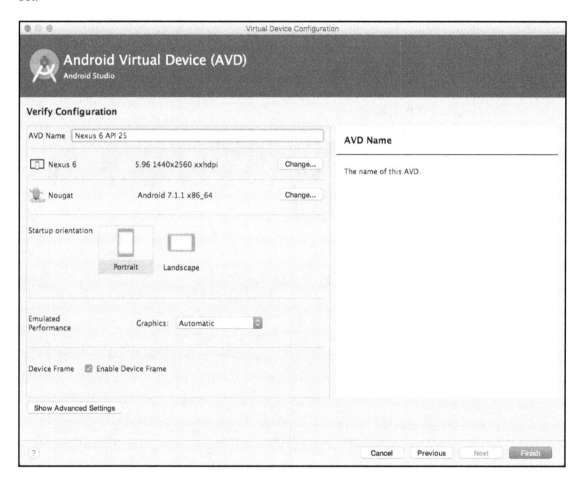

How to set up a real device for developing

It is fine to use an emulator for testing and debugging, but sometimes we really want to test or put the application on a real device. There are a few steps we have to do in order to enable development on our device. First, we need to enable our device for development. We can easily do that by just clicking seven times on the **Settings -> About menu -> Build Number** since Android 4.2. Once we've done this, there will be a new menu option called **Developer options**. We have multiple options there that we can explore, but what we need right now is to enable **USB debugging**.

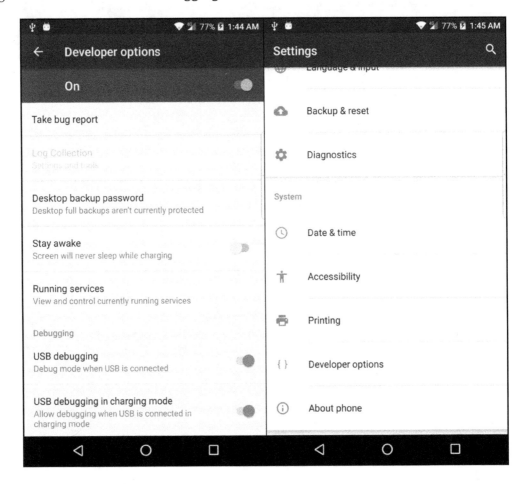

If **USB debugging** is enabled, we'll see our device and running emulators on the device selection:

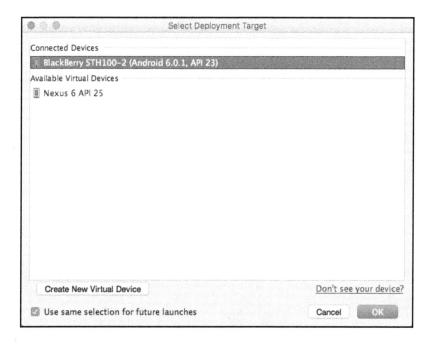

Creating our own first custom view

Now that we have set up our environment and we can run and debug Android applications on both an emulator and a real device, we can start creating our own first custom view. To keep it simple, we will first easily modify an existing view and we will proceed, later on, to create our own view from scratch.

Extending a view

Using the example from the previous section, or just creating a new project with an **Empty Activity** if you've skipped it, we will change the TextView with our own implementation.

If we take a look at the default layout XML file, usually called `activity_main.xml` if you haven't changed it during project creation, we can see there is `TextView` inside a `RelativeLayout`:

```xml
<?xml version="1.0" encoding="utf-8"?>
<RelativeLayout xmlns:android="http://schemas.android.com/apk/res/android"
    xmlns:tools="http://schemas.android.com/tools"
    android:id="@+id/activity_main"
    android:layout_width="match_parent"
    android:layout_height="match_parent"
    android:paddingBottom="@dimen/activity_vertical_margin"
    android:paddingLeft="@dimen/activity_horizontal_margin"
    android:paddingRight="@dimen/activity_horizontal_margin"
    android:paddingTop="@dimen/activity_vertical_margin"
    tools:context="com.packt.rrafols.customview.MainActivity">

    <TextView
        android:layout_width="wrap_content"
        android:layout_height="wrap_content"
        android:text="Hello World!" />
</RelativeLayout>
```

Let's change that `TextView` to a custom class that we will implement just after this:

```xml
<com.packt.rrafols.customview.OwnTextView
        android:layout_width="wrap_content"
        android:layout_height="wrap_content"
        android:text="Hello World!" />
```

We've used the `com.packt.rrafols.customview` package, but please change it accordingly to the package name of your application.

To implement this class, we will first create our class that extends `TextView`:

```java
package com.packt.rrafols.customview;

import android.content.Context;
import android.util.AttributeSet;
import android.widget.TextView;

public class OwnTextView extends TextView {

    public OwnTextView(Context context, AttributeSet attributeSet) {
        super(context, attributeSet);
    }
}
```

This class, or custom view, will behave like a standard `TextView`. Take into consideration the constructor we've used. There are other constructors, but we'll focus only on this one for now. It is important to create it as it'll receive the context and the parameters we defined on the XML layout file.

At this point we're only passing through the parameters and not doing anything fancy with them, but let's prepare our custom view to handle new functionality by overriding the `onDraw()` method:

```
@Override
protected void onDraw(Canvas canvas) {
    super.onDraw(canvas);
}
```

By overriding the `onDraw()` method we're now in control of the drawing cycle of the custom view. If we run the application, we'll not notice any difference from the original example as we haven't added any new behavior or functionality yet. In order to fix this, let's do a very simple change that will prove to us that it is actually working.

On the `onDraw()` method, we'll draw a red rectangle covering the whole area of the view as follows:

```
@Override
    protected void onDraw(Canvas canvas) {
        canvas.drawRect(0, 0, getWidth(), getHeight(), backgroundPaint);
        super.onDraw(canvas);
    }
```

We can use the `getWidth()` and `getHeight()` methods to get the width and height respectively of the view. To define the color and style we'll initialize a new `Paint` object, but we'll do it on the constructor, as it is a bad practice to do it during the `onDraw()` method. We'll cover more about performance later in this book:

```
private Paint backgroundPaint;

    public OwnTextView(Context context, AttributeSet attributeSet) {
        super(context, attributeSet);

        backgroundPaint= new Paint();
        backgroundPaint.setColor(0xffff0000);
        backgroundPaint.setStyle(Paint.Style.FILL);
    }
```

Here, we've initialized the `Paint` object to a red color using integer hexadecimal encoding and set the style to `Style.FILL` so it will fill the whole area. By default, `Paint` style is set to `FILL`, but it doesn't hurt to specifically set it for extra clarity.

If we run the application now, we'll see the `TextView`, which is our own class right now, with a red background as follows:

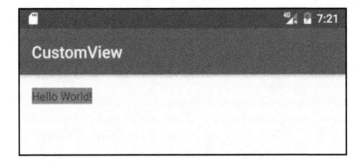

The following code snippet is the whole implementation of the `OwnTextView` class. For more details, check the `Example01` folder in the GitHub repository for the full project:

```
package com.packt.rrafols.customview;

import android.content.Context;
import android.graphics.Canvas;
import android.graphics.Paint;
import android.util.AttributeSet;
import android.widget.TextView;

public class OwnTextView extends TextView {

    private Paint backgroundPaint;

    public OwnTextView(Context context, AttributeSet attributeSet) {
        super(context, attributeSet);

        backgroundPaint = new Paint();
        backgroundPaint.setColor(0xffff0000);
        backgroundPaint.setStyle(Paint.Style.FILL);
    }

    @Override
    protected void onDraw(Canvas canvas) {
        canvas.drawRect(0, 0, getWidth(), getHeight(),
        backgroundPaint);
        super.onDraw(canvas);
```

```
        }
    }
```

This example is only to show how we can extend a standard view and implement our own behaviors; there are multiple other ways in Android to set a background color or to draw a background color to a widget.

Creating a simple view from scratch

Now that we've seen how to modify an already existing View, we'll see a more complex example: how to create our own custom view from scratch!

Let's start by creating an empty class that extends from View:

```
package com.packt.rrafols.customview;

import android.content.Context;
import android.util.AttributeSet;
import android.view.View;

public class OwnCustomView extends View {
    public OwnCustomView(Context context, AttributeSet attributeSet) {
        super(context, attributeSet);
    }
}
```

We will now add the same code as the previous example to draw a red background:

```
package com.packt.rrafols.customview;

import android.content.Context;
import android.graphics.Canvas;
import android.graphics.Paint;
import android.util.AttributeSet;
import android.view.View;

public class OwnCustomView extends View {

    private Paint backgroundPaint;

    public OwnCustomView(Context context, AttributeSet attributeSet) {
        super(context, attributeSet);

        backgroundPaint= new Paint();
        backgroundPaint.setColor(0xffff0000);
        backgroundPaint.setStyle(Paint.Style.FILL);
```

```
        }

        @Override
        protected void onDraw(Canvas canvas) {
            canvas.drawRect(0, 0, getWidth(), getHeight(),
            backgroundPaint);
            super.onDraw(canvas);
        }
    }
```

If we run the application, as we can see in the following screenshot, we'll have a slightly different result from the previous example. This is because in our previous example the `TextView` widget was resizing to the size of the text. If we remember correctly, we had `android:layout_width="wrap_content"` and `android:layout_height="wrap_content"` in our layout XML file. This new custom view we've just created doesn't know how to calculate its size.

Check the `Example02` folder in the GitHub repository for the full implementation of this simple example.

Summary

In this chapter, we have seen the reasoning behind why we might want to build custom views and layouts, but also, that we have to apply common sense. Android provides a great basic framework for creating UIs and not using it would be a mistake. Not every component, button, or widget has to be completely custom developed, but by doing it so in the right spot, we can add an extra feature that might make our application remembered. Also, we've shown some examples of applications that are already in the market and they're using custom views, so we know we are not alone out there! Finally, we've seen how to set up the environment to get ourselves started and we began taking our own first baby steps on custom views.

In the next chapter, we'll keep adding features; we'll see how to calculate the right size of our custom view and learn more about custom rendering.

2
Implementing Your First Custom View

In the previous chapter, we've seen how to create the foundations of a custom view, but unless we add some more features and customizations it'll be pretty useless. In this chapter, we'll continue building on top of these foundations, see how we can parameterize our custom view to allow either ourselves or any other developer to customize them, and at the end, cover some rendering that will enable us to build slightly more complex custom views.

In addition, as we've mentioned in the previous chapter, we can create custom layouts as well. In this chapter, we'll see how to create a simple custom layout.

In more detail, we'll cover the following topics:

- Measuring and parameterizing our custom view
- Instantiating custom views
- Creating custom layouts
- Basic rendering

Measuring and parameterizing our custom view

In order to have a good reusable custom view, it needs to be able to adapt to different sizes and device resolutions, and to increase its reusability even more it should support parameterization.

Measuring our custom view

In the quick example we built in the previous chapter, we delegated all sizes and measurement to the parent view itself. To be honest, we haven't even delegated it; we just didn't do anything specifically to take care of that. Being able to control the size and dimensions of our custom view is something we definitely need to pay some attention to. To start, we're going to **override** the onMeasure() method from view as follows:

```
@Override
protected void onMeasure(int widthMeasureSpec, int heightMeasureSpec) {
    super.onMeasure(widthMeasureSpec, heightMeasureSpec);
}
```

Reading the Android documentation about the onMeasure() method, we should see we must **call** either setMeasuredDimension(int, int) or the superclass' onMeasure(int, int). If we forget to do so, we'll get an IllegalStateException:

```
com.packt.rrafols.customview E/AndroidRuntime: FATAL EXCEPTION: main
Process: com.packt.rrafols.customview, PID: 13601
java.lang.IllegalStateException: View with id -1:
com.packt.rrafols.customview.OwnCustomView#onMeasure() did not set the
measured dimension by calling setMeasuredDimension() at
android.view.View.measure(View.java:18871)
```

There are three different **modes** in which our view's parent can indicate to our view how it should calculate its size. We can get the mode by using the MeasureSpec.getMode(int) method with each size spec widthMeasureSpec and heightMeasureSpec.

These modes are as follows:

- MeasureSpec.EXACTLY
- MeasureSpec.AT_MOST
- MeasureSpec.UNSPECIFIED

We'll get MeasureSpec.EXACTLY when the size has been calculated or decided by the parent. Our view will have that size even if it requires or returns a different size. If we get MeasureSpec.AT_MOST we have more flexibility: we can be as big as we need but up to the size we also have. Finally, if we received MeasureSpec.UNSPECIFIED, we can size our view to whatever size we want or the view needs.

Using MeasureSpec.getSize(int), we can also get a size value from the size spec.

Now that we have all this, how do we know which values map to the width and height parameters on our XML layout file? Easy to see, let's check. For example, if we specify precise values as shown in the `activity_main.xml` file in the GitHub repository, we will get the following code:

```
<com.packt.rrafols.customview.OwnCustomView
    android:layout_width="150dp"
    android:layout_height="150dp"/>
```

Code on our custom view, using `MeasureSpec.toString(int)` to get a string description of the measure specification and the size looks like this:

```
@Override
protected void onMeasure(int widthMeasureSpec, int heightMeasureSpec) {
    Log.d(TAG, "width spec: " +
    MeasureSpec.toString(widthMeasureSpec));
    Log.d(TAG, "height spec: " +
    MeasureSpec.toString(heightMeasureSpec));
    super.onMeasure(widthMeasureSpec, heightMeasureSpec);
}
```

The result on the Android log is as follows:

```
D/com.packt.rrafols.customview.OwnCustomView: width : MeasureSpec: EXACTLY
394
D/com.packt.rrafols.customview.OwnCustomView: height: MeasureSpec: EXACTLY
394
```

Our view will be 394 by 394 pixels exactly. The 394 pixels comes from transforming the 150dp to pixels on the mobile device I was using for testing.

 As there are many Android devices with different resolutions and screen densities, we should always use **density-independent pixel (dp)** or (**dip**) instead of pixels.

For more details about dp, refer to a video by Google available on YouTube: **DesignBytes: Density-independent Pixels**.

If you would like to convert from dp to real pixels on a specific device, you can use the following method:

```
public final int dpToPixels(int dp) {
    return (int) (dp * getResources().getDisplayMetrics().density +
    0.5);
}
```

We can see how the conversion is done using the density of the screen, so on different devices the conversion can be different. The + 0.5 in the previous code is just to round up the value when converting from a floating point number to an int.

To convert from pixels to density-independent points, we have to do the inverse operation, as shown in the following code:

```
public final int pixelsToDp(int dp) {
    return (int) (dp / getResources().getDisplayMetrics().density +
    0.5);
}
```

Let's now see what we receive if we use different measure parameters, such as match_parent or wrap_content, as shown in the activity_main.xml file in the GitHub repository:

```
<com.packt.rrafols.customview.OwnCustomView
    android:layout_width="match_parent"
    android:layout_height="match_parent"/>
```

Running the same code as before, we get the following on the Android log:

```
D/com.packt.rrafols.customview.OwnCustomView: width : MeasureSpec: EXACTLY
996
D/com.packt.rrafols.customview.OwnCustomView: height: MeasureSpec: EXACTLY
1500
```

So we are still getting a MeasureSpec.EXACTLY, but this time with the size of the parent RelativeLayout; let's try changing one of the match_parents for a wrap_content in activity_main.xml:

```
<com.packt.rrafols.customview.OwnCustomView
    android:layout_width="match_parent"
    android:layout_height="wrap_content"/>
```

The result is as follows:

```
D/com.packt.rrafols.customview.OwnCustomView: width : MeasureSpec: EXACTLY
996
D/com.packt.rrafols.customview.OwnCustomView: height: MeasureSpec: AT_MOST
1500
```

We can spot an easy-to-follow pattern with MeasureSpec.EXACTLY and MeasureSpec.AT_MOST, but what about MeasureSpec.UNSPECIFIED?

We'll get a MeasureSpec.UNSPECIFIED if our parent is not bounded; for example, if we have a vertical LinearLayout inside a ScrollView, as shown in the scrollview_layout.xml file in the GitHub repository:

```xml
<?xml version="1.0" encoding="utf-8"?>
<ScrollView xmlns:android="http://schemas.android.com/apk/res/android"
    android:orientation="vertical"
    android:layout_width="match_parent"
    android:layout_height="match_parent">

    <LinearLayout
        android:layout_width="match_parent"
        android:layout_height="wrap_content"
        android:orientation="vertical"
        android:padding="@dimen/activity_vertical_margin">
        <com.packt.rrafols.customview.OwnCustomView
        android:layout_width="match_parent"
        android:layout_height="wrap_content"/>
    </LinearLayout>
</ScrollView>
```

Then we'll get the following on the Android log:

```
D/com.packt.rrafols.customview.OwnCustomView: width : MeasureSpec: EXACTLY
996
D/com.packt.rrafols.customview.OwnCustomView: height: MeasureSpec:
UNSPECIFIED 1500
```

That seems alright, but what happens if we now run this code? We'll get an empty screen; our red background we've previously implemented is gone:

That is because we're not managing the size of our custom view. Let's fix that, as shown in the following code:

```
private static int getMeasurementSize(int measureSpec, int defaultSize) {
        int mode = MeasureSpec.getMode(measureSpec);
        int size = MeasureSpec.getSize(measureSpec);
        switch(mode) {
            case MeasureSpec.EXACTLY:
                return size;

            case MeasureSpec.AT_MOST:
                return Math.min(defaultSize, size);

            case MeasureSpec.UNSPECIFIED:
            default:
                return defaultSize;
        }
    }


    @Override
```

```
protected void onMeasure(int widthMeasureSpec, int
    heightMeasureSpec) {
    int width = getMeasurementSize(widthMeasureSpec, DEFAULT_SIZE);
    int height = getMeasurementSize(heightMeasureSpec,
    DEFAULT_SIZE);
    setMeasuredDimension(width, height);
}
```

Now, depending on the measurement specs, we'll set the size of our view by calling the `setMeasuredDimension(int, int)` method.

For the full example, check the source code in the `Example03-Measurement` folder in the GitHub repository.

Parameterizing our custom view

We have our custom view that adapts to multiple sizes now; that's good, but what happens if we need another custom view that paints the background blue instead of red? And yellow? We shouldn't have to copy the custom view class for each customization. Luckily, we can set parameters on the XML layout and read them from our custom view:

1. First, we need to define the type of parameters we will use on our custom view. We've got to create a file called `attrs.xml` in the `res` folder:

   ```xml
   <?xml version="1.0" encoding="utf-8"?>
   <resources>
       <declare-styleable name="OwnCustomView">
           <attr name="fillColor" format="color"/>
       </declare-styleable>
   </resources>
   ```

2. Then, we add a different namespace on our layout file where we want to use this new parameter we've just created:

   ```xml
   <?xml version="1.0" encoding="utf-8"?>
   <ScrollView
   xmlns:android="http://schemas.android.com/apk/res/android"
       xmlns:app="http://schemas.android.com/apk/res-auto"
       android:orientation="vertical"
       android:layout_width="match_parent"
       android:layout_height="match_parent">

       <LinearLayout
           android:layout_width="match_parent"
           android:layout_height="wrap_content"
   ```

```
                android:orientation="vertical"
                android:padding="@dimen/activity_vertical_margin">

                <com.packt.rrafols.customview.OwnCustomView
                    android:layout_width="match_parent"
                    android:layout_height="wrap_content"
                    app:fillColor="@android:color/holo_blue_dark"/>
        </LinearLayout>
    </ScrollView>
```

3. Now that we have this defined, let's see how we can read it from our custom view class:

```
int fillColor;
TypedArray ta =
    context.getTheme().obtainStyledAttributes(attributeSet,
        R.styleable.OwnCustomView, 0, 0);
try {
    fillColor =
        ta.getColor(R.styleable.OwnCustomView_ocv_fillColor,
            DEFAULT_FILL_COLOR);
} finally {
    ta.recycle();
}
```

By getting a `TypedArray` using the styled attribute ID Android tools created for us after saving the `attrs.xml` file, we'll be able to query for the value of those parameters set on the XML layout file.

In this example, we created an attribute named `fillColor` that will be formatted as a color. This format, or basically, the type of the attribute, is very important to limit the kind of values we can set, and how these values can be retrieved afterwards from our custom view.

Also, for each parameter we define, we'll get a `R.styleable.<name>_<parameter_name>` index in the `TypedArray`. In the preceding code, we're querying for the `fillColor` using the `R.styleable.OwnCustomView_fillColor` index.

 We shouldn't forget to recycle the `TypedArray` after using it so it can be reused later on, but once recycled, we can't use it again.

Let's see the results of this little customization:

We've used color in this specific case, but we can use many other types of parameters; for example:

- Boolean
- Int
- Float
- Color
- Dimension
- Drawable
- String
- Resource

Each one has its own getter method: `getBoolean(int index, boolean defValue)` or `getFloat(int index, float defValue)`.

In addition, to know if a parameter is set we can use the `hasValue(int)` method before querying or we can simply use the default values of the getters. If the attribute is not set at that index, the getter will return the default value.

For the full example, check the `Example04-Parameters` folder in the GitHub repository.

Instantiating custom views

Now that we've seen how to set parameters on the XML layout and parse them on our custom view class, we'll see how to instantiate custom views from code as well and reuse then as much as possible from both instantiation mechanisms.

Instantiating custom views from code

On our custom view, we've created a single constructor with two parameters, a `Context` and an `AttributeSet`. Now, if we're creating our UI programmatically, or if by any other reason we need to instantiate our custom view by code, we need to create an additional constructor.

As we want to keep using our custom view in our XML layouts, we have to keep both constructors. To code avoid duplication, we will create some helper methods to initialize it and use them from both constructors:

```java
public OwnCustomView(Context context) {
    super(context);
    init(DEFAULT_FILL_COLOR);
}

public OwnCustomView(Context context, AttributeSet attributeSet) {
    super(context, attributeSet);

    int fillColor;

    TypedArray ta =
    context.getTheme().obtainStyledAttributes(attributeSet,
    R.styleable.OwnCustomView, 0, 0);
    try {
        fillColor = ta.getColor(R.styleable.OwnCustomView_fillColor,
        DEFAULT_FILL_COLOR);
    } finally {
        ta.recycle();
    }
```

```
            init(fillColor);
    }

    private void init(int fillColor) {
        backgroundPaint = new Paint();
        backgroundPaint.setStyle(Paint.Style.FILL);

        setFillColor(fillColor);
    }

    public void setFillColor(int fillColor) {
        backgroundPaint.setColor(fillColor);
    }
```

We also created a public method, setFillColor(int), so we can set the fill color by code as well. For example, let's modify our Activity to create the view hierarchy programmatically instead of inflating it from an XML layout file:

```
public class MainActivity extends AppCompatActivity {
    private static final int BRIGHT_GREEN = 0xff00ff00;
    @Override
    protected void onCreate(Bundle savedInstanceState) {
        super.onCreate(savedInstanceState);

        LinearLayout linearLayout = new LinearLayout(this);
        linearLayout.setLayoutParams(
                new LinearLayout.LayoutParams(ViewGroup.
                    LayoutParams.MATCH_PARENT,
                    ViewGroup.LayoutParams.MATCH_PARENT));

        OwnCustomView customView = new OwnCustomView(this);
        customView.setFillColor(BRIGHT_GREEN);
        linearLayout.addView(customView);

        setContentView(linearLayout);
    }
}
```

Here, we're just creating a LinearLayout with vertical orientation and adding a custom view as a child. Then we're setting the LinearLayout as the content view of the Activity. Also, we've used a hexadecimal color directly. If we're not used to specifying colors in hexadecimal format, we could use Color.argb() or Color.rgb() to convert color components to an integer value.

The full source code can be found in the Example05-Code folder in the GitHub repository.

Builder pattern

In the previous example, we used the `setFillColor()` method to set the fill color of the custom view, but suppose we will have many other parameters, the code might get a bit messy with all the setters.

Let's create a simple example: instead of having one single background color, we'll have four different colors and we'll draw a gradient on our view:

Let's start by defining the four different colors and their setters as follows:

```java
private int topLeftColor = DEFAULT_FILL_COLOR;
private int bottomLeftColor = DEFAULT_FILL_COLOR;
private int topRightColor = DEFAULT_FILL_COLOR;
private int bottomRightColor = DEFAULT_FILL_COLOR;
private boolean needsUpdate = false;

public void setTopLeftColor(int topLeftColor) {
    this.topLeftColor = topLeftColor;
    needsUpdate = true;
}

public void setBottomLeftColor(int bottomLeftColor) {
    this.bottomLeftColor = bottomLeftColor;
    needsUpdate = true;
}

public void setTopRightColor(int topRightColor) {
    this.topRightColor = topRightColor;
    needsUpdate = true;
}

public void setBottomRightColor(int bottomRightColor) {
    this.bottomRightColor = bottomRightColor;
    needsUpdate = true;
}
```

We also added a boolean to check if we have to update the gradient. Let's ignore thread synchronization here as it's not the main purpose of this example.

Then, we've added a check for this `boolean` on the `onDraw()` method and, in the case it's needed, it'll regenerate the gradient:

```java
@Override
protected void onDraw(Canvas canvas) {
    if (needsUpdate) {
        int[] colors = new int[] {topLeftColor, topRightColor,
```

```
        bottomRightColor, bottomLeftColor};

        LinearGradient lg = new LinearGradient(0, 0, getWidth(),
            getHeight(), colors, null, Shader.TileMode.CLAMP);
        backgroundPaint.setShader(lg);
        needsUpdate = false;
    }

    canvas.drawRect(0, 0, getWidth(), getHeight(), backgroundPaint);
    super.onDraw(canvas);
}
```

It's a bad practice to create new object instances on the `onDraw()` method. Here it is only done once, or every time we're changing the colors. If we were changing the color constantly, this would be a bad example as it'll be constantly creating new objects, polluting the memory, and triggering the **Garbage Collector (GC)**. There will be more on performance and memory in `Chapter 7`, *Performance Considerations*.

We have to update the code of our `Activity` to set these new colors:

```
public class MainActivity extends AppCompatActivity {
    private static final int BRIGHT_GREEN = 0xff00ff00;
    private static final int BRIGHT_RED = 0xffff0000;
    private static final int BRIGHT_YELLOW = 0xffffff00;
    private static final int BRIGHT_BLUE = 0xff0000ff;

    @Override
    protected void onCreate(Bundle savedInstanceState) {
        super.onCreate(savedInstanceState);

        LinearLayout linearLayout = new LinearLayout(this);
        linearLayout.setLayoutParams(
                new LinearLayout.LayoutParams(ViewGroup.
                LayoutParams.MATCH_PARENT,
                ViewGroup.LayoutParams.MATCH_PARENT));

        OwnCustomView customView = new OwnCustomView(this);
        customView.setTopLeftColor(BRIGHT_RED);
        customView.setTopRightColor(BRIGHT_GREEN);
        customView.setBottomLeftColor(BRIGHT_YELLOW);
        customView.setBottomRightColor(BRIGHT_BLUE);
        linearLayout.addView(customView);
        setContentView(linearLayout);
    }
}
```

As we can see, we've used four setters to set the colors. If we've got more parameters, we could use more setters, but one of the issues of this approach is that we have to take care of thread synchronization and the object might be in an unstable state until all calls are done.

Another option is to add all the parameters to the constructor, but that is not a good solution either. It'd make our job more complex, as it'll be hard to remember the order of the parameters or, in the case where we had optional, to create many different constructors or passing null references that make our code harder to read and maintain.

Check the full source code of this example in the `Example06-BuilderPattern-NoBuilder` folder of the GitHub repository.

Now that we've introduced the issue, let's solve it by implementing the `Builder` pattern on our custom view. We start by creating a `public static class` inside our custom view that will build it as follows:

```
public static class Builder {
    private Context context;
    private int topLeftColor = DEFAULT_FILL_COLOR;
    private int topRightColor = DEFAULT_FILL_COLOR;
    private int bottomLeftColor = DEFAULT_FILL_COLOR;
    private int bottomRightColor = DEFAULT_FILL_COLOR;

    public Builder(Context context) {
        this.context = context;
    }

    public Builder topLeftColor(int topLeftColor) {
        this.topLeftColor = topLeftColor;
        return this;
    }

    public Builder topRightColor(int topRightColor) {
        this.topRightColor = topRightColor;
        return this;
    }

    public Builder bottomLeftColor(int bottomLeftColor) {
        this.bottomLeftColor = bottomLeftColor;
        return this;
    }

    public Builder bottomRightColor(int bottomRightColor) {
        this.bottomRightColor = bottomRightColor;
        return this;
    }
```

```
    public OwnCustomView build() {
        return new OwnCustomView(this);
    }
}
```

We also create a new private constructor that only accepts an `OwnCustomView.Builder`
object:

```
private OwnCustomView(Builder builder) {
    super(builder.context);

    backgroundPaint = new Paint();
    backgroundPaint.setStyle(Paint.Style.FILL);

    colorArray = new int[] {
            builder.topLeftColor,
            builder.topRightColor,
            builder.bottomRightColor,
            builder.bottomLeftColor
    };

    firstDraw = true;
}
```

We've removed other constructors for clarity. Also at this point, we create the array of
colors based on the colors that the `builder` object has and a `boolean` to know if it's the first
time it'll be drawn or not.

This will be useful to instantiate the `LinearGradient` object only once and avoid creating
many instances:

```
@Override
    protected void onDraw(Canvas canvas) {
        if (firstDraw) {
            LinearGradient lg = new LinearGradient(0, 0, getWidth(),
            getHeight(),
                    colorArray, null, Shader.TileMode.CLAMP);

            backgroundPaint.setShader(lg);
            firstDraw = false;
        }

        canvas.drawRect(0, 0, getWidth(), getHeight(),
        backgroundPaint);
        super.onDraw(canvas);
    }
```

Now, once the object is created we can't change its colors, but we don't have to worry about thread synchronization and the object's state.

To make it work, let's update the code on our `Activity` as well:

```
public class MainActivity extends AppCompatActivity {
    private static final int BRIGHT_GREEN = 0xff00ff00;
    private static final int BRIGHT_RED = 0xffff0000;
    private static final int BRIGHT_YELLOW = 0xffffff00;
    private static final int BRIGHT_BLUE = 0xff0000ff;
    @Override
    protected void onCreate(Bundle savedInstanceState) {
        super.onCreate(savedInstanceState);

        LinearLayout linearLayout = new LinearLayout(this);
        linearLayout.setLayoutParams(
                new LinearLayout.LayoutParams(ViewGroup.
                LayoutParams.MATCH_PARENT,
                ViewGroup.LayoutParams.MATCH_PARENT));

        OwnCustomView customView = new OwnCustomView.Builder(this)
                .topLeftColor(BRIGHT_RED)
                .topRightColor(BRIGHT_GREEN)
                .bottomLeftColor(BRIGHT_YELLOW)
                .bottomRightColor(BRIGHT_BLUE)
                .build();

        linearLayout.addView(customView);

        setContentView(linearLayout);
    }
}
```

Using the `Builder` pattern, our code is cleaner and the object is constructed or built when we've set all the properties and this will become even handier if the custom view has more parameters.

The full example source code can be found in the `Example07-BuilderPattern` folder in the GitHub repository.

Creating a custom layout

Android provides several layouts to position our views in many different ways, but if these standard layouts aren't useful for our specific use case, we can create our own layouts.

Extending ViewGroup

The process to create a custom layout is quite similar to creating a custom view. We've got to create a class that extends from ViewGroup instead of view, create the appropriate constructors, implement the onMeasure() method, and override the onLayout() method rather than the onDraw() method.

Let's create a very simple custom layout; it will add elements to the right of the previous element until it doesn't fit on the screen, then it'll start a new row, using the higher element to calculate where this new row will start and avoid any overlapping between views.

Adding random sized views, where each view has a red background, will look as follows:

First, let's create a class that extends from `ViewGroup`:

```
public class CustomLayout extends ViewGroup {

    public CustomLayout(Context context, AttributeSet attrs) {
        super(context, attrs);
    }

    @Override
    protected void onLayout(boolean changed, int l, int t, int r, int b) {

    }
}
```

We created the constructor and we implemented the `onLayout()` method as it's an abstract method and we've got to implement it. Let's add some logic to it:

```
@Override
    protected void onLayout(boolean changed, int l, int t, int r, int b){
            int count = getChildCount();
            int left = l + getPaddingLeft();
            int top = t + getPaddingTop();

            // keeps track of maximum row height
            int rowHeight = 0;

            for (int i = 0; i < count; i++) {
                View child = getChildAt(i);

                int childWidth = child.getMeasuredWidth();
                int childHeight = child.getMeasuredHeight();

                // if child fits in this row put it there
                if (left + childWidth < r - getPaddingRight()) {
                    child.layout(left, top, left + childWidth, top +
                    childHeight);
                    left += childWidth;
            } else {
                // otherwise put it on next row
                    left = l + getPaddingLeft();
                    top += rowHeight;
                    rowHeight = 0;
            }

                // update maximum row height
                if (childHeight > rowHeight) rowHeight = childHeight;
            }
        }
```

This logic implements what we've described before; it tries to add a child to the right of the previous child and if it doesn't fit on the layout width, checking the current `left` position plus the measured child width, it starts a new row. The `rowHeight` variable measures the higher view on that row.

Let's also implement the `onMeasure()` method:

```
@Override
protected void onMeasure(int widthMeasureSpec, int heightMeasureSpec) {
    int count = getChildCount();

    int rowHeight = 0;
    int maxWidth = 0;
    int maxHeight = 0;
    int left = 0;
    int top = 0;

    for (int i = 0; i < count; i++) {
        View child = getChildAt(i);
        measureChild(child, widthMeasureSpec, heightMeasureSpec);

        int childWidth = child.getMeasuredWidth();
        int childHeight = child.getMeasuredHeight();

        // if child fits in this row put it there
        if (left + childWidth < getWidth()) {
            left += childWidth;
        } else {
            // otherwise put it on next row
            if(left > maxWidth) maxWidth = left;
            left = 0;
            top += rowHeight;
            rowHeight = 0;
        }

        // update maximum row height
        if (childHeight > rowHeight) rowHeight = childHeight;
    }

    if(left > maxWidth) maxWidth = left;
    maxHeight = top + rowHeight;

    setMeasuredDimension(getMeasure(widthMeasureSpec, maxWidth),
    getMeasure(heightMeasureSpec, maxHeight));

}
```

The logic is the same as before, but it's not laying out its children. It calculates the maximum width and height that will be needed, and then with the help of a helper method sets the dimensions of this custom layout according to the width and height measurement specs:

```java
private int getMeasure(int spec, int desired) {
        switch(MeasureSpec.getMode(spec)) {
            case MeasureSpec.EXACTLY:
                return MeasureSpec.getSize(spec);

            case MeasureSpec.AT_MOST:
                return Math.min(MeasureSpec.getSize(spec), desired);

            case MeasureSpec.UNSPECIFIED:
            default:
                return desired;
        }
    }
```

Now that we've got our custom layout, let's add it to our `activity_main` layout:

```xml
<?xml version="1.0" encoding="utf-8"?>
<RelativeLayout xmlns:android="http://schemas.android.com/apk/res/android"
    xmlns:tools="http://schemas.android.com/tools"
    android:id="@+id/activity_main"
    android:layout_width="match_parent"
    android:layout_height="match_parent"
    android:padding="@dimen/activity_vertical_margin"
    tools:context="com.packt.rrafols.customview.MainActivity">

    <com.packt.rrafols.customview.CustomLayout
        android:id="@+id/custom_layout"
        android:layout_width="match_parent"
        android:layout_height="match_parent">

    </com.packt.rrafols.customview.CustomLayout>
</RelativeLayout>
```

For the last step, let's add some random sized views to it:

```java
public class MainActivity extends AppCompatActivity {
    @Override
    protected void onCreate(Bundle savedInstanceState) {
        super.onCreate(savedInstanceState);
        setContentView(R.layout.activity_main);

        CustomLayout customLayout = (CustomLayout)
        findViewById(R.id.custom_layout);
```

```
Random rnd = new Random();
for(int i = 0; i < 50; i++) {
    OwnCustomView view = new OwnCustomView(this);

    int width = rnd.nextInt(200) + 50;
    int height = rnd.nextInt(100) + 100;
    view.setLayoutParams(new ViewGroup.LayoutParams(width,
    height));
    view.setPadding(2, 2, 2, 2);

    customLayout.addView(view);
}
    }
}
```

Check the `Example08-CustomLayout` folder on GitHub for the full source code of this example.

On this page, we can also find a quite complex example of a full-featured custom layout.

Basic rendering

So far we've only been drawing a solid background or a linear gradient. That's neither exciting nor really useful. Let's see how we can draw more interesting shapes and primitives. We'll do so by creating an example of a circular activity indicator that we'll be adding more and more features to in the following chapters.

Creating the basic circular activity indicator

The `Canvas` class provides us with many drawing functions; for example:

- `drawArc()`
- `drawBitmap()`
- `drawOval()`
- `drawPath()`

To draw a circular activity indicator, we can use the `drawArc()` method. Let's create the basic class and draw an arc:

```java
public class CircularActivityIndicator extends View {
    private static final int DEFAULT_FG_COLOR = 0xffff0000;
    private static final int DEFAULT_BG_COLOR = 0xffa0a0a0;
    private Paint foregroundPaint;
    private int selectedAngle;

    public CircularActivityIndicator(Context context, AttributeSet
    attributeSet) {
        super(context, attributeSet);

        foregroundPaint = new Paint();
        foregroundPaint.setColor(DEFAULT_FG_COLOR);
        foregroundPaint.setStyle(Paint.Style.FILL);
        selectedAngle = 280;
    }

    @Override
    protected void onDraw(Canvas canvas) {
        canvas.drawArc(
                0,
                0,
                getWidth(),
                getHeight(),
                0, selectedAngle, true, foregroundPaint);
    }
}
```

The result is as shown in the following screenshot:

Let's fix the ratio, so the width of the arc will be the same as the height:

```
@Override
protected void onDraw(Canvas canvas) {
    int circleSize = getWidth();
    if (getHeight() < circleSize) circleSize = getHeight();

    int horMargin = (getWidth() - circleSize) / 2;
    int verMargin = (getHeight() - circleSize) / 2;

    canvas.drawArc(
            horMargin,
            verMargin,
            horMargin + circleSize,
            verMargin + circleSize,
            0, selectedAngle, true, foregroundPaint);
}
```

We'll use the smaller dimension, either width or height, and draw the arc centered with a square ratio: with the same width and same height.

This doesn't look like an activity indicator; let's change it and draw only a thin band of the arc. We can achieve this by using the clipping capabilities that canvas gives us. We can use canvas.clipRect or canvas.clipPath, for example. When using clipping methods, we can also specify a clipping operation. By default, if we don't specify it, it will intersect with the current clipping.

To draw only a thin band, we'll create a smaller arc in a path, around *75%* of the size of the arc we'd like to draw. Then, we'll subtract it from the clipping rectangle of the whole view:

```java
private Path clipPath;

@Override
protected void onDraw(Canvas canvas) {
    int circleSize = getWidth();
    if (getHeight() < circleSize) circleSize = getHeight();

    int horMargin = (getWidth() - circleSize) / 2;
    int verMargin = (getHeight() - circleSize) / 2;

    // create a clipPath the first time
    if(clipPath == null) {
        int clipWidth = (int) (circleSize * 0.75);

        int clipX = (getWidth() - clipWidth) / 2;
        int clipY = (getHeight() - clipWidth) / 2;
        clipPath = new Path();
        clipPath.addArc(
                clipX,
                clipY,
                clipX + clipWidth,
                clipY + clipWidth,
                0, 360);
    }

    canvas.clipRect(0, 0, getWidth(), getHeight());
    canvas.clipPath(clipPath, Region.Op.DIFFERENCE);

    canvas.drawArc(
            horMargin,
            verMargin,
            horMargin + circleSize,
            verMargin + circleSize,
            0, selectedAngle, true, foregroundPaint);
}
```

In the following screenshot, we can see the difference:

As finishing touches, let's add a background color to the arc and change the starting position to the top of the view.

To draw the background, we'll add the following code to create a background `Paint` to our constructor:

```
backgroundPaint = new Paint();
backgroundPaint.setColor(DEFAULT_BG_COLOR);
backgroundPaint.setStyle(Paint.Style.FILL);
```

Then modify the `onDraw()` method to actually draw it, just before drawing the other arc:

```
canvas.drawArc(
        horMargin,
        verMargin,
        horMargin + circleSize,
        verMargin + circleSize,
        0, 360, true, backgroundPaint);
```

As a small difference, we're drawing the whole 360 degrees so it will cover the whole circle.

To change the starting position of the arc, we'll rotate our drawing operations. Canvas supports rotation, translation, and matrix transformations as well. In this case, we only need to rotate 90 degrees anti-clockwise to get our starting point at the top of the arc:

```java
@Override
protected void onDraw(Canvas canvas) {
    int circleSize = getWidth();
    if (getHeight() < circleSize) circleSize = getHeight();

    int horMargin = (getWidth() - circleSize) / 2;
    int verMargin = (getHeight() - circleSize) / 2;

    // create a clipPath the first time
    if(clipPath == null) {
        int clipWidth = (int) (circleSize * 0.75);

        int clipX = (getWidth() - clipWidth) / 2;
        int clipY = (getHeight() - clipWidth) / 2;
        clipPath = new Path();
        clipPath.addArc(
                clipX,
                clipY,
                clipX + clipWidth,
                clipY + clipWidth,
                0, 360);
    }

    canvas.clipRect(0, 0, getWidth(), getHeight());
    canvas.clipPath(clipPath, Region.Op.DIFFERENCE);

    canvas.save();
    canvas.rotate(-90, getWidth() / 2, getHeight() / 2);

    canvas.drawArc(
            horMargin,
            verMargin,
            horMargin + circleSize,
            verMargin + circleSize,
            0, 360, true, backgroundPaint);

    canvas.drawArc(
            horMargin,
            verMargin,
            horMargin + circleSize,
            verMargin + circleSize,
```

```
            0, selectedAngle, true, foregroundPaint);

        canvas.restore();
    }
```

We also used `canvas.save()` and `canvas.restore()` to preserve the state of our canvas; otherwise, it will be rotating -90 degrees each time it is drawn. When calling the `canvas.rotate()` method, we also specified the center point of the rotation, which matches with the center point of the screen and the center point of the arc.

Whenever we're using a `canvas` function as `rotate`, `scale`, or `translate`, for example, we're actually applying a transformation to all the successive `canvas` drawing operations.

The final result is shown in the following screenshot:

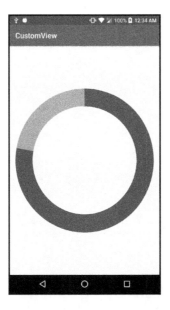

Something we need to be aware of is that not all `canvas` operations are supported by hardware on all Android versions. Please check if the operations you have to do are supported or provide a runtime workaround for them. Find more information about what operations are hardware accelerated at:

`https://developer.android.com/guide/topics/graphics/hardware-accel.html.`

Here is the final implementation of the class:

```java
public class CircularActivityIndicator extends View {
    private static final int DEFAULT_FG_COLOR = 0xffff0000;
    private static final int DEFAULT_BG_COLOR = 0xffa0a0a0;
    private Paint backgroundPaint;
    private Paint foregroundPaint;
    private int selectedAngle;
    private Path clipPath;

    public CircularActivityIndicator(Context context, AttributeSet
        attributeSet) {
        super(context, attributeSet);

        backgroundPaint = new Paint();
        backgroundPaint.setColor(DEFAULT_BG_COLOR);
        backgroundPaint.setStyle(Paint.Style.FILL);

        foregroundPaint = new Paint();
        foregroundPaint.setColor(DEFAULT_FG_COLOR);
        foregroundPaint.setStyle(Paint.Style.FILL);

        selectedAngle = 280;
    }

    @Override
    protected void onDraw(Canvas canvas) {
        int circleSize = getWidth();
        if (getHeight() < circleSize) circleSize = getHeight();

        int horMargin = (getWidth() - circleSize) / 2;
        int verMargin = (getHeight() - circleSize) / 2;

        // create a clipPath the first time
        if(clipPath == null) {
            int clipWidth = (int) (circleSize * 0.75);

            int clipX = (getWidth() - clipWidth) / 2;
            int clipY = (getHeight() - clipWidth) / 2;
            clipPath = new Path();
            clipPath.addArc(
                    clipX,
                    clipY,
                    clipX + clipWidth,
                    clipY + clipWidth,
                    0, 360);
        }
```

```
        canvas.clipPath(clipPath, Region.Op.DIFFERENCE);

        canvas.save();
        canvas.rotate(-90, getWidth() / 2, getHeight() / 2);

        canvas.drawArc(
                horMargin,
                verMargin,
                horMargin + circleSize,
                verMargin + circleSize,
                0, 360, true, backgroundPaint);

        canvas.drawArc(
                horMargin,
                verMargin,
                horMargin + circleSize,
                verMargin + circleSize,
                0, selectedAngle, true, foregroundPaint);

        canvas.restore();
    }
}
```

The whole example source code can be found in the `Example09-BasicRendering` folder in the GitHub repository.

Furthermore, I gave a talk about this at the Android Developer's Backstage in Krakow in January 2015; here is a link to the presentation:

`https://www.slideshare.net/RaimonRls/android-custom-views-72600098`.

Summary

In this chapter, we have seen how to measure and how to add parameters to our custom view. We also saw how to instantiate a custom view from code and use a `Builder` pattern to simplify all the parameters and keep our code cleaner. In addition, we went through a quick example of a custom layout and we started building a circular activity indicator. In the next chapter, we will see how to handle events and add some interactions to the circular activity indicator we've just started to build.

3
Handling Events

Now that we've seen the basics of canvas drawing and we've our custom view adapted to its size, it's time to interact with it. Many custom views will only need to draw something in a special way; that's the reason we created them as custom views, but many others will need to react to user events. For example, how our custom view will behave when the user clicks or drags on top of it?

To answer these questions, we'll cover with more detail the following points in this chapter:

- Basic event handling
- Advanced event handling

Basic event handling

Let's start by adding some basic event handling to our custom views. We'll go through the basics, and we'll add more complex events later on.

Reacting to touch events

In order to make our custom view interactive, one of the first things we will implement is to process and react to touch events, or basically, when the user touches or drags on top of our custom view.

Android provides us with the `onTouchEvent()` method that we can override in our custom view. By overriding this method, we'll get any touch event happening on top of it. To see how it works, let's add it to the custom view we built in the last chapter:

```
@Override
public boolean onTouchEvent(MotionEvent event) {
    Log.d(TAG, "touch: " + event);
    return super.onTouchEvent(event);
}
```

Lets also add a log call to see the events we receive. If we run this code and touch on top of our view, we'll get the following:

```
D/com.packt.rrafols.customview.CircularActivityIndicator: touch:
MotionEvent { action=ACTION_DOWN, actionButton=0, id[0]=0, x[0]=644.3645,
y[0]=596.55804, toolType[0]=TOOL_TYPE_FINGER, buttonState=0, metaState=0,
flags=0x0, edgeFlags=0x0, pointerCount=1, historySize=0,
eventTime=30656461, downTime=30656461, deviceId=9, source=0x1002 }
```

As we can see, there is a lot of information on the event, coordinates, action type, and time, but even if we perform more actions on it, we'll only get `ACTION_DOWN` events. That's because the default implementation of view is not clickable. By default, if we don't enable the clickable flag on the view, the default implementation of `onTouchEvent()` will return false and ignore further events.

The `onTouchEvent()` method has to return `true` if the event has been processed or false if it hasn't. If we receive an event in our custom view and we don't know what to do or we're not interested in such events, we should return `false`, so it can be processed by our view's parent or by any other component or the system.

To receive more types of events, we can do two things:

- Set the view as clickable using `setClickable(true)`
- Implement our own logic and process the events in our custom class

Later on, we'll implement more complex events; we'll go for the second option.

Lets carry out a quick test and change the method to return simply true instead of calling the parent method:

```
@Override
public boolean onTouchEvent(MotionEvent event) {
    Log.d(TAG, "touch: " + event);
    return true;
}
```

Now, we should receive many other types of events, as follows:

```
...CircularActivityIndicator: touch: MotionEvent { action=ACTION_DOWN,
...CircularActivityIndicator: touch: MotionEvent { action=ACTION_UP,
...CircularActivityIndicator: touch: MotionEvent { action=ACTION_DOWN,
...CircularActivityIndicator: touch: MotionEvent { action=ACTION_MOVE,
...CircularActivityIndicator: touch: MotionEvent { action=ACTION_MOVE,
...CircularActivityIndicator: touch: MotionEvent { action=ACTION_MOVE,
...CircularActivityIndicator: touch: MotionEvent { action=ACTION_UP,
...CircularActivityIndicator: touch: MotionEvent { action=ACTION_DOWN,
```

As seen in the preceding example, we can see that in the previous log we not only have both ACTION_DOWN and ACTION_UP but also ACTION_MOVE to indicate that we're performing an action of drag on top of our view.

We'll focus on handling the ACTION_UP and ACTION_DOWN events first. Let's add a boolean variable name that will keep track whether we're currently pressing or touching our view or not:

```
private boolean pressed;

public CircularActivityIndicator(Context context, AttributeSet
attributeSet) {
    ...
    ...
    pressed = false;
}
```

We've added the variable and set its default state to false, as the view will not be pressed when created. Now, lets add the code to handle this on our onTouchEvent() implementation:

```
@Override
public boolean onTouchEvent(MotionEvent event) {
    Log.d(TAG, "touch: " + event);
    switch(event.getAction()) {
        case MotionEvent.ACTION_DOWN:
            pressed = true;
            return true;

        case MotionEvent.ACTION_UP:
            pressed = false;
            return true;

        default:
            return false;
```

```
        }
    }
```

We're processed the `MotionEvent`. The `ACTION_DOWN` and `MotionEvent.ACTION_UP` events; any other action we receive here, we ignore and return `false`, since we haven't handled it.

OK, now we've a variable that keeps track if we're pressing our view or not, but we should do something else or otherwise this won't be of that much use. Let's modify the `onDraw()` method to paint the circle in a different color when the view is pressed:

```
private static final int DEFAULT_FG_COLOR = 0xffff0000;
private static final int PRESSED_FG_COLOR = 0xff0000ff;
@Override
protected void onDraw(Canvas canvas) {
    if (pressed) {
        foregroundPaint.setColor(PRESSED_FG_COLOR);
    } else {
        foregroundPaint.setColor(DEFAULT_FG_COLOR);
    }
```

If we run this example and we touch our view, we'll see that nothing happens! What is the issue? We're not triggering any repaint or redraw event and the view it's not drawn again. We can see this code is working if we manage to keep pressing the view and put the app in the background and return it to the foreground, for example. However, to do it properly, we should trigger a repaint event when we change something that requires our view to be redrawn, as follows:

```
@Override
public boolean onTouchEvent(MotionEvent event) {
    Log.d(TAG, "touch: " + event);
    switch(event.getAction()) {
        case MotionEvent.ACTION_DOWN:
            pressed = true;
            invalidate();
            return true;

        case MotionEvent.ACTION_UP:
            pressed = false;
            invalidate();
            return true;

        default:
            pressed = false;
            invalidate();
```

```
            return false;
        }
    }
```

OK, that should do the trick! Calling the invalidate method will trigger an `onDraw()` method call in the future:
`https://developer.android.com/reference/android/view/View.html#invalidate()`.

We can now refactor this code and move it into a method:

```
    private void changePressedState(boolean pressed) {
        this.pressed = pressed;
        invalidate();
    }

    @Override
    public boolean onTouchEvent(MotionEvent event) {
        Log.d(TAG, "touch: " + event);
        switch(event.getAction()) {
            case MotionEvent.ACTION_DOWN:
                changePressedState(true);
                return true;

            case MotionEvent.ACTION_UP:
                changePressedState(false);
                return true;

            default:
                changePressedState(false);
                return false;
        }
    }
```

We need to be aware that invalidate has to be called from the UI thread and will throw an exception if called from another thread. If we've to call it from another thread, for example, we've to update a view after receiving some data from a web service, we've to call `postInvalidate()`.

Here is the result:

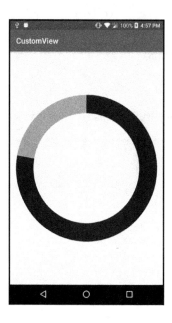

Drag events

Now that we're already reacting to ACTION_DOWN and ACTION_UP events, we will add a bit more complexity by reacting to ACTION_MOVE as well.

Let's update the angle, based on the amount of dragging in both directions. To do so, we need to store where the user pressed in the first place, so we'll store the variables lastX and lastY with the X and Y coordinates on the ACTION_DOWN event.

When we receive an ACTION_MOVE event, we calculate the difference between the lastX and lastY coordinates and the current values we received with the event. We update selectedAngle with the average of the X and Y difference, and we finally update the lastX and lastY coordinates. We have to remember to call invalidate or otherwise our view will not be redrawn:

```
private float lastX, lastY;

@Override
public boolean onTouchEvent(MotionEvent event) {
    switch(event.getAction()) {
        case MotionEvent.ACTION_DOWN:
```

```
            changePressedState(true);

            lastX = event.getX();
            lastY = event.getY();
            return true;

        case MotionEvent.ACTION_UP:
            changePressedState(false);
            return true;

        case MotionEvent.ACTION_MOVE:
            float dragX = event.getX();
            float dragY = event.getY();

            float dx = dragX - lastX;
            float dy = dragY - lastY;

            selectedAngle += (dx + dy) / 2;

            lastX = dragX;
            lastY = dragY;

            invalidate();
            return true;

        default:
            return false;
    }
}
```

That movement might feel a bit unnatural, so if we want the angle of the circle to follow where we actually pressed, we should change from Cartesian coordinates to polar coordinates:
https://en.wikipedia.org/wiki/List_of_common_coordinate_transformations.

With this change, there is no need to track the previous coordinates, so we can replace our code with the following:

```
private int computeAngle(float x, float y) {
    x -= getWidth() / 2;
    y -= getHeight() / 2;

    int angle = (int) (180.0 * Math.atan2(y, x) / Math.PI) + 90;
    return (angle > 0) ? angle : 360 + angle;
}

@Override
public boolean onTouchEvent(MotionEvent event) {
```

```
switch(event.getAction()) {
    case MotionEvent.ACTION_DOWN:
        selectedAngle = computeAngle(event.getX(), event.getY());
        changePressedState(true);
        return true;

    case MotionEvent.ACTION_UP:
        changePressedState(false);
        return true;

    case MotionEvent.ACTION_MOVE:
        selectedAngle = computeAngle(event.getX(), event.getY());
        invalidate();
        return true;

    default:
        return false;
    }
}
```

Complex layouts

So far, we've seen how to manage `onTouchEvent()` events on our custom view, but that was on a view occupying the whole screen size, so it was a bit of a simple approach. If we want to include or view inside a `ViewGroup` that also handles touch events, for example, a `ScrollView`, what do we've to change?

Let's change the layout for this one:

```xml
<?xml version="1.0" encoding="utf-8"?>
<RelativeLayout xmlns:android="http://schemas.android.com/apk/res/android"
    xmlns:tools="http://schemas.android.com/tools"
    android:id="@+id/activity_main"
    android:layout_width="match_parent"
    android:layout_height="match_parent"
    android:padding="@dimen/activity_vertical_margin"
    tools:context="com.packt.rrafols.customview.MainActivity">

    <ScrollView
        android:layout_width="match_parent"
        android:layout_height="wrap_content"
        android:layout_alignParentTop="true"
        android:layout_alignParentStart="true"
        android:layout_marginTop="13dp">

        <LinearLayout
```

```
    android:layout_width="match_parent"
    android:layout_height="wrap_content"
    android:orientation="vertical">

<TextView
    android:layout_width="match_parent"
    android:layout_height="wrap_content"
    android:paddingTop="100dp"
    android:paddingBottom="100dp"
    android:text="Top"
    android:background="@color/colorPrimaryDark"
    android:textColor="@android:color/white"
    android:gravity="center"/>

<com.packt.rrafols.customview.CircularActivityIndicator
    android:layout_width="match_parent"
    android:layout_height="300dp"/>

<TextView
    android:layout_width="match_parent"
    android:layout_height="wrap_content"
    android:paddingTop="100dp"
    android:paddingBottom="100dp"
    android:text="Bottom"
    android:background="@color/colorPrimaryDark"
    android:textColor="@android:color/white"
    android:gravity="center"/>
    </LinearLayout>
  </ScrollView>
</RelativeLayout>
```

Basically, we've put our custom view inside `ScrollView`, so both can process events. We should be selective in which events have to be processed by our view and have to be processed by which the `ScrollView`.

To do so, the view provides us with the `getParent()` method, to get its parent: `https://developer.android.com/reference/android/view/ViewParent.html`.

Once we've the parent, we can call `requestDisallowInterceptTouchEvent` to disallow the parent and its parents to intercept touch events. In addition, to only consume the events we're interested in, we added a check to see if the location where the user touched is inside the radius of the circle or outside. If the touch is outside, we'll ignore the event and won't process it.

```
private boolean computeAndSetAngle(float x, float y) {
    x -= getWidth() / 2;
    y -= getHeight() / 2;
```

```
        double radius = Math.sqrt(x * x + y * y);
        if(radius > circleSize/2) return false;

        int angle = (int) (180.0 * Math.atan2(y, x) / Math.PI) + 90;
        selectedAngle = ((angle > 0) ? angle : 360 + angle);
        return true;
    }

    @Override
    public boolean onTouchEvent(MotionEvent event) {
        boolean processed;

        switch(event.getAction()) {
            case MotionEvent.ACTION_DOWN:
                processed = computeAndSetAngle(event.getX(), event.getY());
                if(processed) {
                    getParent().requestDisallowInterceptTouchEvent(true);
                    changePressedState(true);
                }
                return processed;

            case MotionEvent.ACTION_UP:
                getParent().requestDisallowInterceptTouchEvent(false);
                changePressedState(false);
                return true;

            case MotionEvent.ACTION_MOVE:
                processed = computeAndSetAngle(event.getX(), event.getY());
                invalidate();
                return processed;

            default:
                return false;
        }
    }
```

We compute the radius applying the same Cartesian to the polar transformation we used before. We also changed the code, so if the touch is inside the radius of the circle, we call getParent().requestDisallowInterceptTouchEvent(true) on the ACTION_DOWN event, telling the ViewParent to not intercept the touch events. We need to undo this action by calling the opposite getParent().requestDisallowInterceptTouchEvent(false) on the ACTION_UP event.

This is the result of this change, and we can see that there is a `TextView` view on top and another one at the bottom of our custom view:

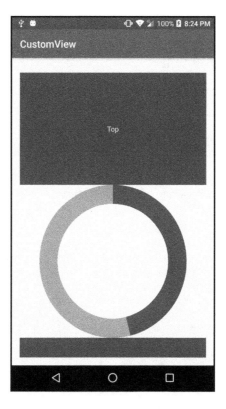

Now if we touch on the circle, our custom view will only process the event and change the circle angle. On the other hand, touching just outside the circle we'll let the `ScrollView` process the events.

There aren't that many changes, but when building a custom view that can potentially be reused in multiple places, we should definitely test it on multiple layout configurations to see how it behaves.

Find the full source code of this example in the `Example10-Events` folder in the GitHub repository.

Advanced event handling

We've seen how to process `onTouchEvent()`, but we can also detect some **gestures** or more complex interactions. Android provides us with the `GestureDetector` to help us detect some gestures. There is even a `GestureDetectorCompat` on the support library to provide this support to older versions of Android.

For more information on the `GestureDetector`, please check the Android documentation.

Detecting gestures

Let's change the code we've been building to use `GestureDetector`. We'll also use a `Scroller` implementation to scroll smoothly between values. We can modify the constructor to create the `Scroller` object and the `GestureDetector` with an implementation of a `GestureDetector.OnGestureListener`:

```
private GestureDetector gestureListener;
private Scroller angleScroller;

public CircularActivityIndicator(Context context, AttributeSet
attributeSet) {
    super(context, attributeSet);

    ...
    selectedAngle = 280;
    pressed = false;

    angleScroller = new Scroller(context, null, true);
    angleScroller.setFinalX(selectedAngle);

    gestureListener = new GestureDetector(context, new
GestureDetector.OnGestureListener() {
      boolean processed;

      @Override
      public boolean onDown(MotionEvent event) {
          processed = computeAndSetAngle(event.getX(), event.getY());
          if (processed) {
              getParent().requestDisallowInterceptTouchEvent(true);
              changePressedState(true);
              postInvalidate();
          }
          return processed;
      }
```

```
@Override
public void onShowPress(MotionEvent e) {

}

@Override
public boolean onSingleTapUp(MotionEvent e) {
    endGesture();
    return false;
}

@Override
public boolean onScroll(MotionEvent e1, MotionEvent e2, float
distanceX, float distanceY) {
    computeAndSetAngle(e2.getX(), e2.getY());
    postInvalidate();
    return true;
}

@Override
public void onLongPress(MotionEvent e) {
    endGesture();
}

@Override
public boolean onFling(MotionEvent e1, MotionEvent e2, float
velocityX, float velocityY) {
    return false;
}
        });
    }
```

There are many callbacks in this interface, but first, in order to process the gestures, we need to return true on the onDown() callback; otherwise, we're indicating that we will not process the chain of events further.

We've simplified onTouchEvent() now, as it just simply forwards the event to the gestureListener:

```
@Override
public boolean onTouchEvent(MotionEvent event) {
    return gestureListener.onTouchEvent(event);
}
```

As we may have different gestures, long press, flings, scrolls, we created a method to end the gesture and restore the status:

```
private void endGesture() {
    getParent().requestDisallowInterceptTouchEvent(false);
    changePressedState(false);
    postInvalidate();
}
```

We've modified the `computeAndSetAngle()` method to use `Scroller`:

```
private boolean computeAndSetAngle(float x, float y) {
    x -= getWidth() / 2;
    y -= getHeight() / 2;

    double radius = Math.sqrt(x * x + y * y);
    if(radius > circleSize/2) return false;

    int angle = (int) (180.0 * Math.atan2(y, x) / Math.PI) + 90;
    angle = ((angle > 0) ? angle : 360 + angle);

    if(angleScroller.computeScrollOffset()) {
        angleScroller.forceFinished(true);
    }

    angleScroller.startScroll(angleScroller.getCurrX(), 0, angle -
    angleScroller.getCurrX(), 0);
    return true;
}
```

The `Scroller` instance will be animating the values; we need to keep checking the updated values to perform the animation. One approach to do so will be to check on the `onDraw()` method if the animation is finished and trigger an invalidate in order to redraw the view if it isn't:

```
@Override
protected void onDraw(Canvas canvas) {
    boolean notFinished = angleScroller.computeScrollOffset();
    selectedAngle = angleScroller.getCurrX();

    ...

    if (notFinished) invalidate();
}
```

The `computeScrollOffset()` will return true if the `Scroller` hasn't reached the end; also after calling it, we can query the value of the scroll using the `getCurrX()` method. In this example, we're animating the value of the circle angle, but we're using the X coordinate of the `Scroller` to animate it.

Using this `GestureDetector`, we can also detect long presses and flings, for example. As flings involve more animations, we'll cover it in the following chapters of this book.

For more information about how to make views interactive refer to:
`https://developer.android.com/training/custom-views/making-interactive.html`.

The source code of this example can be found in the `Example11-Events` folder, in the GitHub repository.

Summary

In this chapter, we've seen how to interact with our custom views. A part of the power of building custom views is the ability to interact with them and make them interactive. We have also seen how to simply react to touch and release events, how to drag elements and calculate the delta distance between drag events, and finally how to use `GestureDetector`.

As rendering has been kept quite simple until now, we'll focus on making our rendering more complex and using more drawing primitives in the next chapter.

4
Advanced 2D Rendering

Being able to draw more complex primitives or use a composition of them is critical to making the user experience of our custom view awesome, useful, and special. So far, we've been using some drawing and rendering operations on our custom view, but if we check the Android documentation closely, that's a much reduced set of what Android provides to developers. We have drawn some primitives, saved and restored our `canvas` state, and applied some clipping operations, but that's only the top thin layer. In this chapter, we'll see these operations again, but we'll also see few new drawing operations and how we can use everything together. We'll cover the following topics in more detail:

- Drawing operations
- Masking and clipping
- Gradients
- Putting it all together

Drawing operations

As we've just mentioned, we have already seen and used some drawing operations, but that was only the envelope of what's inside. We'll see new drawing operations and how to combine them.

Bitmaps

Let's start by drawing bitmaps or images. Instead of having a white background, we'll use an image as background for our custom view. Using the source code from our previous example, we could do some very simple modifications to draw an image:

First, let's define a `Bitmap` object that will hold a reference to the image:

```
private Bitmap backgroundBitmap;
```

To start, let's initialize it with the application icon we already have on our application:

```
public CircularActivityIndicator(Context context, AttributeSet
attributeSet) {
    super(context, attributeSet);
    backgroundBitmap = BitmapFactory.decodeResource(getResources(),
    R.mipmap.ic_launcher);
```

`BitmapFactory` provides us several ways to load and decode images.

Once we have the image loaded, we can draw it on our `onDraw()` method by calling the `drawBitmap(Bitmap bitmap, float left, float top, Paint paint)` method:

```
@Override
protected void onDraw(Canvas canvas) {
    if (backgroundBitmap != null) {
        canvas.drawBitmap(backgroundBitmap, 0, 0, null);
    }
}
```

As we don't need anything special from our `Paint` object, we've set it to `null`; we'll use it later in this book, but for the moment, just ignore it.

If `backgroundBitmap` is `null`, it means that it couldn't load the image; so, for safety, we should always check. This code will just draw the icon on the top-left corner of our custom view, although we could change its position by setting either different coordinates-here we used 0,0-or applying a transformation to our `canvas` like we did before. For example, we can rotate the image based on the angle selected by the user:

```
@Override
protected void onDraw(Canvas canvas) {
    // apply a rotation of the bitmap based on the selectedAngle
    if (backgroundBitmap != null) {
        canvas.save();
        canvas.rotate(selectedAngle, backgroundBitmap.getWidth() / 2,
```

```
            backgroundBitmap.getHeight() / 2);
        canvas.drawBitmap(backgroundBitmap, 0, 0, null);
        canvas.restore();
    }
```

Note that we've added the center of the image as the pivot point, or otherwise will rotate by its top-left corner.

There are other ways to draw images; Android has another method for drawing an image from a source `Rect` to a destination `Rect`. The `Rect` object allows us to store four coordinates and use it as a rectangle.

The method `drawBitmap(Bitmap bitmap, Rect source, Rect dest, Paint paint)` is very useful for drawing a portion of an image into any other size we want. This method will take care of scaling the selected portion of the image to fill the destination rectangle. For example, we could use the following code if we wanted to draw the right half of the image scaled to the whole custom view size.

First, let's define the background `Bitmap` and two `Rect`; one to hold the source dimensions and other for the destination:

```
private Bitmap backgroundBitmap;
private Rect bitmapSource;
private Rect bitmapDest;
```

Then, let's instantiate them on the class constructor. It's not a good practice to do it on the `onDraw()` method, as we should avoid allocating memory to methods that are called on every frame or every time we draw our custom view. Doing so will trigger additional garbage collector cycles and affect performance.

```
public CircularActivityIndicator(Context context, AttributeSet
attributeSet) {
    super(context, attributeSet);

    backgroundBitmap = BitmapFactory.decodeResource(getResources(),
    R.mipmap.ic_launcher);
    bitmapSource = new Rect();

    bitmapSource.top = 0;
    bitmapSource.left = 0;
    if(backgroundBitmap != null) {
        bitmapSource.left = backgroundBitmap.getWidth() / 2;
        bitmapSource.right = backgroundBitmap.getWidth();
        bitmapSource.botto
        m = backgroundBitmap.getHeight();
```

```
        }
        bitmapDest = new Rect();
```

By default, `Rect` initializes the four coordinates to 0 but here, for clarity, we set the top and the left coordinates to 0. If the image was loaded successfully, we set the right and bottom to the width and height of the image, respectively. As we want to draw only the right half of the image only, we update the left border to half the width of the image.

On the `onDraw()` method, we set the right and bottom coordinates of the destination `Rect` to the width and height of the custom view and we draw the image:

```
@Override
protected void onDraw(Canvas canvas) {
    if (backgroundBitmap != null) {
        bitmapDest.right = getWidth();
        bitmapDest.bottom = getHeight();

        canvas.drawBitmap(backgroundBitmap, bitmapSource, bitmapDest,
        null);
    }
}
```

Let's check the result:

We can see it doesn't abide by the aspect ratio of the image, but let's solve it by computing the ratio of the smaller dimension, either horizontal or vertical, and scale it by this ration. Then, apply it to the other dimension. We will see the following code after calculating the image ratio:

```
@Override
protected void onDraw(Canvas canvas) {
    if (backgroundBitmap != null) {
        if ((bitmapSource.width() > bitmapSource.height() && getHeight() >
        getWidth()) ||
            (bitmapSource.width() <= bitmapSource.height() && getWidth() >=
            getHeight())) {
            double ratio = ((double) getHeight()) / ((double)
            bitmapSource.height());
            int scaledWidth = (int) (bitmapSource.width() * ratio);
            bitmapDest.top = 0;
            bitmapDest.bottom = getHeight();
            bitmapDest.left = (getWidth() - scaledWidth) / 2;
            bitmapDest.right = bitmapDest.left + scaledWidth;
        } else {
            double ratio = ((double) getWidth()) / ((double)
            bitmapSource.width());
            int scaledHeight = (int) (bitmapSource.height() * ratio);
            bitmapDest.left = 0;
            bitmapDest.right = getWidth();
            bitmapDest.top = 0;
            bitmapDest.bottom = scaledHeight;
        }
        canvas.drawBitmap(backgroundBitmap, bitmapSource, bitmapDest,
        null);
    }
}
```

We can also draw a `Bitmap` using a transformation `Matrix`. To do so, we can create a new instance of `Matrix` and apply a transformation:

```
private Matrix matrix;
```

Create an instance on the constructor. Do not create an instance on the `onDraw()` instance, as it will pollute the memory and trigger unnecessary garbage collection, as mentioned earlier:

```
matrix = new Matrix();
matrix.postScale(0.2f, 0.2f);
matrix.postTranslate(0, 200);
```

Please be careful with the matrix operation order; there are also post-operations and pre-operations. Check the matrix class documentation for more information.

On the `onDraw()` method, just draw `Bitmap` using the `drawBitmap` (`Bitmap bitmap`, `Matrix matrix`, `Paint paint`) method and using the `matrix` we've initialized on our class constructor. In this example, we also used a `null Paint` object to simplify, as we don't need anything specific from the `Paint` object here.

```
canvas.drawBitmap(backgroundBitmap, matrix, null);
```

Although these are the most common methods to draw a `Bitmap` onto a `Canvas`, there are a few more methods.

Furthermore, check the `Example12-Drawing` folder on the GitHub repository to see the full source code of this example.

Using the Paint class

We've been drawing some primitives until now, but `Canvas` provides us with many more primitive rendering methods. We'll briefly cover some of them, but first, let's first talk about the `Paint` class as we haven't introduced it properly.

According to the official definition, the `Paint` class holds the style and color information about how to draw primitives, text, and bitmaps. If we check the examples we've been building, we created a `Paint` object on our class constructor or on the `onCreate` method, and we used it to draw primitives later on our `onDraw()` method. As, for instance, if we set our background Paint instance `Style` to `Paint.Style.FILL`, it'll fill the primitive, but we can change it to `Paint.Style.STROKE` if we only want to draw the border or the strokes of the silhouette. We can draw both using `Paint.Style.FILL_AND_STROKE`.

To see `Paint.Style.STROKE` in action, we'll draw a black border on top of our selected colored bar in our custom View. Let's start by defining a new `Paint` object called `indicatorBorderPaint` and initialize it on our class constructor:

```
indicatorBorderPaint = new Paint();
indicatorBorderPaint.setAntiAlias(false);
indicatorBorderPaint.setColor(BLACK_COLOR);
indicatorBorderPaint.setStyle(Paint.Style.STROKE);
indicatorBorderPaint.setStrokeWidth(BORDER_SIZE);
indicatorBorderPaint.setStrokeCap(Paint.Cap.BUTT);
```

We also defined a constant with the size of the border line and set the stroke width to this size. If we set the width to 0, Android guaranties it'll use a single pixel to draw the line. As we want to draw a thick black border, this is not our case right now. In addition, we set the stroke Cap to Paint.Cap.BUTT to avoid the stroke overflowing its path. There are two more Caps we can use, Paint.Cap.SQUARE and Paint.Cap.ROUND. These last two will end the stroke, respectively, with a circle, rounding the stroke, or a square.

Let's quickly see the differences between the three Caps and also introduce the drawLine primitive.

First of all, we create an array with all three Caps, so we can easily iterate between them and create a more compact code:

```
private static final Paint.Cap[] caps = new Paint.Cap[] {
        Paint.Cap.BUTT,
        Paint.Cap.ROUND,
        Paint.Cap.SQUARE
};
```

Now, on our onDraw() method, let's draw a line using each of the Caps using the drawLine(float startX, float startY, float stopX, float stopY, Paint paint) method:

```
int xPos = (getWidth() - 100) / 2;
int yPos = getHeight() / 2 - BORDER_SIZE * CAPS.length / 2;
for(int i = 0; i < CAPS.length; i++) {
    indicatorBorderPaint.setStrokeCap(CAPS[i]);
    canvas.drawLine(xPos, yPos, xPos + 100, yPos,
    indicatorBorderPaint);
    yPos += BORDER_SIZE * 2;
}
indicatorBorderPaint.setStrokeCap(Paint.Cap.BUTT);
```

We'll have a result similar to the following image. As we can see, the line is slightly shorter when using the Paint.Cap.BUTT stroke Cap:

Also, as we saw before, we set the `AntiAlias` flag to true on the `Paint` object. If this flag is enabled, all operations that support it will smooth the corners of what they are drawing. Let's compare the differences with this flag enabled and disabled:

On the left, we've the three lines with the `AntiAlias` flag enabled, and on the right, we've the same three lines with the `AntiAlias` flag disabled. We can only appreciate a difference on the rounded edges, but the result is smoother and nicer. Not all operations and primitives support it and might have an impact on performance, so we need to be careful when using this flag.

We can also draw multiple lines using another method called `drawLine(float[] points, int offset, int count, Paint paint)` or its simpler form `drawLine(float[] points, Paint paint)`.

This method will draw a single line for each set of the four entries into the array; it would be like calling `drawLine(array[index], array[index + 1], array[index + 2], array[index +3], paint)`, incrementing the index by 4, and repeating this process until the end of the array.

On the first method, we could also specify the amount of lines to draw and from which offset we start inside the array.

Now, let's go to the task we had and draw the border:

```
canvas.drawArc(
        horMargin + BORDER_SIZE / 4,
        verMargin + BORDER_SIZE / 4,
        horMargin + circleSize - BORDER_SIZE /2,
        verMargin + circleSize - BORDER_SIZE /2,
        0, selectedAngle, true, indicatorBorderPaint);
```

It's simply drawing the same arc, but with this new `Paint`. One small detail: as the border width grows centered from where it's drawing the stroke, we need to reduce the size of the arc by `BORDER_SIZE /2`. Let's see the result:

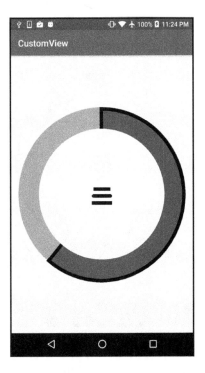

We're missing the inner border, but that's normal because, if we remember from our previous chapters, that part is there because we're clipping it out, not because `drawArc` is drawing it that way. We can do a small trick to draw this internal border. We'll draw another arc with the size of the clipping area, but just the stroke:

```
canvas.drawArc(
        clipX - BORDER_SIZE / 4,
        clipY - BORDER_SIZE / 4,
        clipX + clipWidth + BORDER_SIZE / 2,
        clipY + clipWidth + BORDER_SIZE / 2,
        0, selectedAngle, true, indicatorBorderPaint);
```

Here, we've applied the same logic with the border size, but the other way around: we draw the arc slightly bigger instead of smaller.

Let's see the results:

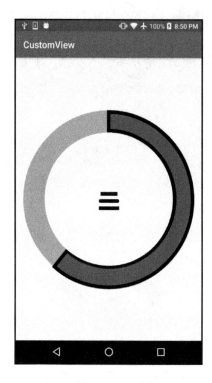

We've mentioned earlier in this book, but it's important not to create new `Paint` objects in the `onDraw()` method or basically, in any method that will be called every time a frame is drawn. We might be tempted as, in some cases, it feels convenient; however, avoid the temptation and create the objects in the class constructor or just reuse the objects. We can change the `Paint` class instance properties and reuse it to paint with different colors or with different styles.

Find the entire source code of this example in the `Example13-Paint` folder on the GitHub repository.

We'll be playing more with the `Paint` object and its properties, but now, let's move to drawing more primitives.

Drawing more primitives

Let's start by the simplest drawing operations: drawColor(int color), drawARGB(int a, int r, int g, int b), drawRGB(int r, int g, int b), and drawPaint(Paint paint). These will fill the entire canvas, taking into account the clipping area.

Let's move forward to drawRect() and drawRoundRect(). These two methods are quite simple too, drawRect() will draw a rectangle and drawRoundRect() will draw a rectangle with rounded borders.

We can use both methods directly, specifying the coordinates or using Rect. Let's create a simple example that will draw a new random rounded rectangle every time the view is drawn or it's onDraw() method is called.

To start, lets define two ArrayLists; one will hold the coordinates and the other will hold the color information of that rectangle:

```
private Paint paint;
private ArrayList<Float> rects;
private ArrayList<Integer> colors;
```

We also declared a Paint object that we'll use to draw all the rounded rectangles. Let's now initialize them:

```
public PrimitiveDrawer(Context context, AttributeSet attributeSet) {
    super(context, attributeSet);

    rects = new ArrayList<>();
    colors = new ArrayList<>();

    paint = new Paint();
    paint.setStyle(Paint.Style.FILL);
    paint.setAntiAlias(true);
}
```

We've set the paint object style to Paint.Style.FILL and set the AntiAlias flag, but we haven't set the color. We'll do so before drawing each rectangle.

Let's now implement our `onDraw()` method. To start, we'll add four new random coordinates. As `Math.random()` returns a value from 0 to 1, we multiply it by the current view width and height to get a proper view coordinate. We also generate a new random color with full opacity:

```
@Override
protected void onDraw(Canvas canvas) {
    canvas.drawColor(BACKGROUND_COLOR);

    int width = getWidth();
    int height = getHeight();

    for (int i = 0; i < 2; i++) {
        rects.add((float) Math.random() * width);
        rects.add((float) Math.random() * height);
    }
    colors.add(0xff000000 | (int) (0xffffff * Math.random()));

    for (int i = 0; i < rects.size() / 4; i++) {
        paint.setColor(colors.get(i));
        canvas.drawRoundRect(
                rects.get(i * 4     ),
                rects.get(i * 4 + 1),
                rects.get(i * 4 + 2),
                rects.get(i * 4 + 3),
                40, 40, paint);
    }

    if (rects.size() < 400) postInvalidateDelayed(20);
}
```

Then, we'll loop with all the random points we added and take the 4 of them at the time, assuming the first two will be the starting X and Y and the latter two will be the ending X and Y coordinates of the rectangle. We hardcoded 40 as the angle of the rounded edges. We can play with this value to change the amount of roundness.

We've introduced bitwise operations on colors. We know we can store a color in a 32-bit integer value, and usually, in ARGB format. That gives us 8 bits for each component. Doing bitwise operations, we can easily manipulate colors. For more information on bitwise operations, please refer to:

`https://en.wikipedia.org/wiki/Bitwise_operation`.

To finish, if we have less than `100` rectangles or `400` coordinates in our array, we post an `Invalidate` event delayed by `20` milliseconds. It is only for demonstration purposes and to show that it is adding and drawing more rectangles. The `drawRoundRect()` method can easily be changed by `drawRect()` by just removing the two hardcoded `40`s as the angle of the rounded edges.

Let's see the result:

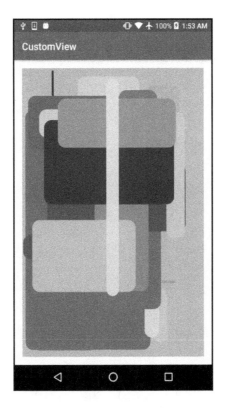

For the full source code, check the `Example14-Primitives-Rect` folder in the GitHub repository.

Let's continue with other primitives, for example, drawPoints. The drawPoints(float[] points, Paint paint) method will simply draw a list of points. It will use the stroke width and the stroke Cap of the paint object. For instance, a quick example that draws few random lines and also draws a point both at the beginning and at the end of each line:

```
@Override
protected void onDraw(Canvas canvas) {
    canvas.drawColor(BACKGROUND_COLOR);

    if (points == null) {
        points = new float[POINTS * 2];
        for(int i = 0; i < POINTS; i++) {
            points[i * 2    ] = (float) Math.random() * getWidth();
            points[i * 2 + 1] = (float) Math.random() * getHeight();
        }
    }

    paint.setColor(0xffa0a0a0);
    paint.setStrokeWidth(4.f);
    paint.setStrokeCap(Paint.Cap.BUTT);
    canvas.drawLines(points, paint);

    paint.setColor(0xffffffff);
    paint.setStrokeWidth(10.f);
    paint.setStrokeCap(Paint.Cap.ROUND);
    canvas.drawPoints(points, paint);
}
```

Let's see the result:

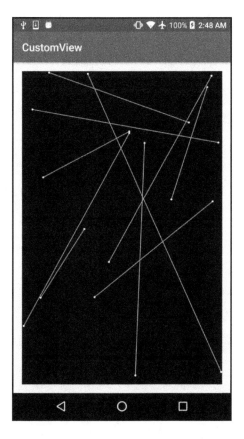

We're creating the points array here on the `onDraw()` method, but it's done only once.

Check the full source code of this example in the `Example15-Primitives-Points` folder, in the GitHub repository.

Building on top of the previous example, we can easily introduce the `drawCircle` primitive. Let's change the code a bit though; instead of generating only pairs of random values, let's generate three random values. The first two will be the X and Y coordinate of the circle and the third the circle's radius. In addition, let's remove the lines for the sake of clarity:

```
@Override
protected void onDraw(Canvas canvas) {
    canvas.drawColor(BACKGROUND_COLOR);

    if (points == null) {
        points = new float[POINTS * 3];
        for(int i = 0; i < POINTS; i++) {
            points[i * 3    ] = (float) Math.random() * getWidth();
            points[i * 3 + 1] = (float) Math.random() * getHeight();
            points[i * 3 + 2] = (float) Math.random() * (getWidth()/4);
        }
    }

    for (int i = 0; i < points.length / 3; i++) {
        canvas.drawCircle(
                points[i * 3    ],
                points[i * 3 + 1],
                points[i * 3 + 2],
                paint);
    }
}
```

We've also initialized our `paint` object on our class constructor:

```
paint = new Paint();
paint.setStyle(Paint.Style.FILL);
paint.setAntiAlias(true);
paint.setColor(0xffffffff);
```

Let's see the result:

Check the full source code of this example on the `Example16-Primitives-Circles` folder, in the GitHub repository.

To find out about all the primitives, modes, and methods to draw on a `Canvas`, check the Android documentation.

Paths can be considered as containers of primitives, lines, curves, and other geometric shapes that, as we already seen, can be used as clipping regions, drawn, or used to draw text on it.

To begin, let's modify our previous example and convert all the circles to a `Path`:

```
@Override
protected void onDraw(Canvas canvas) {
    if (path == null) {
        float[] points = new float[POINTS * 3];
        for(int i = 0; i < POINTS; i++) {
            points[i * 3    ] = (float) Math.random() * getWidth();
            points[i * 3 + 1] = (float) Math.random() * getHeight();
            points[i * 3 + 2] = (float) Math.random() * (getWidth()/4);
        }

        path = new Path();

        for (int i = 0; i < points.length / 3; i++) {
            path.addCircle(
                    points[i * 3    ],
                    points[i * 3 + 1],
                    points[i * 3 + 2],
                    Path.Direction.CW);
        }

        path.close();
    }
```

We don't need to store the points, so we declared it as a local variable. We created a `Path` object instead. Now that we have this `Path` with all the circles in it, we can draw it by calling the `drawPath(Path path, Paint paint)` method or use it as a clipping mask.

We added an image to our project and we'll draw it as a background image, but we'll apply a clipping mask defined by our `Path` to make things interesting:

```
canvas.save();
if (!touching) canvas.clipPath(path);
if(background != null) {
    backgroundTranformation.reset();
    float scale = ((float) getWidth()) / background.getWidth();
    backgroundTranformation.postScale(scale, scale);
    canvas.drawBitmap(background, backgroundTranformation, null);
}
canvas.restore();
}
```

Let's see the result:

To see the full source code of this example, check the `Example17-Paths` folder on the GitHub repository.

Checking the Android documentation about Paths, we can see that there are a lot of methods to add primitives to a `Path`, for example:

- `addCircle()`
- `addRect()`
- `addRoundRect()`
- `addPath()`

However, we're not limited to these methods, we can also add lines or displace where our path will start our next element using the `lineTo` or `moveTo` methods, respectively. In the case we want to use relative coordinates, the `Path` class provides us with the methods `rLineTo` and `rMoveTo` that assumes that the given coordinates are relative from the last point of the `Path`.

For additional information about `Path` and its methods, check the Android documentation website. We can do so, using the methods `cubicTo` and `quadTo`. A Bezier curve consists of control points that control the shape of the smooth curve. Let's build a quick example by adding control points each time the user taps on the screen.

First, let's define two `Paint` objects, one for the Bezier lines and another to draw the control points for reference:

```
pathPaint = new Paint();
pathPaint.setStyle(Paint.Style.STROKE);
pathPaint.setAntiAlias(true);
pathPaint.setColor(0xffffffff);
pathPaint.setStrokeWidth(5.f);

pointsPaint = new Paint();
pointsPaint.setStyle(Paint.Style.STROKE);
pointsPaint.setAntiAlias(true);
pointsPaint.setColor(0xffff0000);
pointsPaint.setStrokeCap(Paint.Cap.ROUND);
pointsPaint.setStrokeWidth(40.f);
```

Control points will be drawn as round red dots, while the Bezier lines will be drawn as thinner white lines. As we're initializing our objects, let's also define an empty `Path` and a float array to store the points:

```
points = new ArrayList<>();
path = new Path();
```

Now, let's override `onTouchEvent()` to add the point where the user tapped the screen and trigger a redraw of our custom view by calling the invalidate method.

```
@Override
public boolean onTouchEvent(MotionEvent event) {
    if (event.getAction() == MotionEvent.ACTION_DOWN) {
        points.add(event.getX());
        points.add(event.getY());

        invalidate();
    }

    return super.onTouchEvent(event);
}
```

On our `onDraw()` method, let's first check if we have already three points. If that is the case, let's add a cubic Bezier to our `Path`:

```
while(points.size() - currentIndex >= 6) {
    float x1 = points.get(currentIndex);
    float y1 = points.get(currentIndex + 1);

    float x2 = points.get(currentIndex + 2);
    float y2 = points.get(currentIndex + 3);

    float x3 = points.get(currentIndex + 4);
    float y3 = points.get(currentIndex + 5);

    if (currentIndex == 0) path.moveTo(x1, y1);
    path.cubicTo(x1, y1, x2, y2, x3, y3);
    currentIndex += 6;
}
```

The `currentIndex` maintains the last index of the point array that has been inserted into the `Path`.

Now, let's draw the `Path` and the points:

```
canvas.drawColor(BACKGROUND_COLOR);
canvas.drawPath(path, pathPaint);

for (int i = 0; i < points.size() / 2; i++) {
    float x = points.get(i * 2     );
    float y = points.get(i * 2 + 1);
    canvas.drawPoint(x, y, pointsPaint);
}
```

Let's see the result:

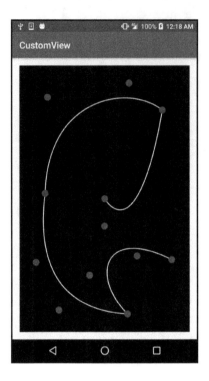

See the full source code of this example on the `Example18-Paths` folder, in the GitHub repository.

Drawing text

Text can be considered a primitive from the point of view of `Canvas` operations, but we've put it here on its own section, as it's quite important. Instead of starting with the simplest example, as we've just introduced Paths, we'll continue our previous example and draw the text on top of the `Path`. To draw the text, we'll reuse the `Paint` object for the Bezier curve, but we'll add some text parameters:

```
pathPaint.setTextSize(50.f);
pathPaint.setTextAlign(Paint.Align.CENTER);
```

This sets the size of the text and also aligns it to the center of the Path, so every time we add new points, the text position will adapt to remain at the center. To draw the text, we simply call the drawTextOnPath() method:

```
canvas.drawTextOnPath("Building Android UIs with Custom Views", path, 0, 0,
pathPaint);
```

This was a very quick addition to our code, but if we execute our application, we can see the results with the text over the Path lines:

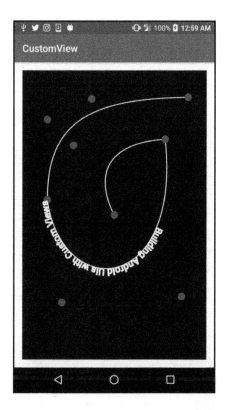

Take into account that we're drawing the same things as we drawn before, but we can freely use the Path just as the guide for the text. There is no need to draw it or to draw the control points.

Check the full source code of this example on the Example19-Text folder, in the GitHub repository.

We've started drawing text on Paths, as we had the example almost built. However, there are more simple methods for drawing text. For instance, we can just draw a text on a specific position of the screen by calling either `canvas.drawText(String text, float x, float y, Paint paint)` or `canvas.drawText(char[] text, float x, float y, Paint paint)`.

These methods will just do their job, but they will not check if the text fits in the available space and they will definitely not split and wrap the text. To do so, we'll have to do it ourselves. The `Paint` class provides us with methods to measure text and calculate text boundaries. For example, we created a small helper method that returns the width and height of `String`:

```
private static final float[] getTextSize(String str, Paint paint) {
    float[] out = new float[2];
    Rect boundaries = new Rect();
    paint.getTextBounds(str, 0, str.length(), boundaries);

    out[0] = paint.measureText(str);
    out[1] = boundaries.height();
    return out;
}
```

We've used the text boundary to get the text height, but we've used the `measureText()` method to get the text width. There are some differences on how the size is computed in both methods. Although it's not currently properly documented on the Android documentation site, there is an old discussion about this on Stack Overflow: http://stackoverflow.com/questions/7549182/android-paint-measuretext-vs-gettext bounds.

However, we shouldn't implement our own text splitting method. If we want to draw a large text and we know it might need splitting and wrapping, we can use the `StaticLayout` class. In the example here, we'll create a `StaticLayout` with the width of half the view width.

We can implement it on our `onLayout()` method:

```
@Override
protected void onLayout(boolean changed, int left, int top, int right, int
bottom) {
    super.onLayout(changed, left, top, right, bottom);

    // create a layout of half the width of the View
    if (layout == null) {
        layout = new StaticLayout(
                LONG_TEXT,
                0,
                LONG_TEXT.length(),
                paint,
                (right - left) / 2,
                Layout.Alignment.ALIGN_NORMAL,
                1.f,
                1.f,
                true);
    }
}
```

In our `onDraw()` method, we draw it centered on the screen. As we know, the layout width was half the view width; we know we have to displace it by a quarter of the width.

```
@Override
protected void onDraw(Canvas canvas) {
    canvas.drawColor(BACKGROUND_COLOR);

    canvas.save();
    // center the layout on the View
    canvas.translate(canvas.getWidth()/4, 0);
    layout.draw(canvas);
    canvas.restore();
}
```

Here is the result:

Check the full source code of this example in the `Example20-Text` folder, in the GitHub repository.

Transformations and operations

We already used some `canvas` transformations on our custom view before, but let's revisit the `Canvas` operations we can use. First of all, let's see how we can concatenate these transformations. Once we've used a transformation, any other transformation we use will be concatenated or applied on top of our previous operations. To avoid this behavior, we've to call the `save()` and `restore()` methods we also used before. To see how transformations build on top of each other, let's create a simple example.

First, let's create a `paint` object on our constructor:

```
public PrimitiveDrawer(Context context, AttributeSet attributeSet) {
    super(context, attributeSet);

    paint = new Paint();
    paint.setStyle(Paint.Style.STROKE);
    paint.setAntiAlias(true);
    paint.setColor(0xffffffff);
}
```

Now, let's calculate the rectangle size based on the size of the screen on the `onLayout()` method:

```
@Override
 protected void onLayout(boolean changed, int left, int top, int right,
 int bottom) {
    super.onLayout(changed, left, top, right, bottom);

    int smallerDimension = (right - left);
    if (bottom - top < smallerDimension) smallerDimension = bottom -
    top;

    rectSize = smallerDimension / 10;
    timeStart = System.currentTimeMillis();
}
```

We also stored the starting time, which we will use it for a quick and simple animation afterwards. Now, we're ready to implement the `onDraw()` method:

```
@Override
protected void onDraw(Canvas canvas) {
    float angle = (System.currentTimeMillis() - timeStart) / 100.f;

    canvas.drawColor(BACKGROUND_COLOR);

    canvas.save();
    canvas.translate(canvas.getWidth() / 2, canvas.getHeight() / 2);

    for (int i = 0; i < 15; i++) {
        canvas.rotate(angle);
        canvas.drawRect(-rectSize / 2, -rectSize / 2, rectSize / 2,
        rectSize / 2, paint);
        canvas.scale(1.2f, 1.2f);
    }
```

```
        canvas.restore();
        invalidate();
    }
```

We've first calculated the `angle` based on the amount of time that passed since the beginning. Animations should always be based on time and not on the amount of frames drawn.

Then, we draw the background, store the `canvas` state by calling `canvas.save()`, and perform a translation to the center of the screen. We'll base all transformations and drawings from the center, instead of the top left corner.

In this example, we'll draw 15 rectangles where each one will be increasingly rotated and scaled. As transformations are applied on top of each other, this is very easy to do in a simple `for()` loop. It is important to draw the rectangle from `-rectSize / 2` to `rectSize / 2` instead of `0` to `rectSize`; otherwise, it will be rotating from one angle.

Change the code line where we draw the rectangle to `canvas.drawRect(0, 0, rectSize, rectSize, paint)` to see what happens.

There is, though, an alternative to this method: we can use pivot points on the transformations. Both `rotate()` and `scale()` methods support two additional `float` parameters that are the pivot point coordinates. If we look at the source code implementation of `scale(float sx, float sy, float px, float py)`, we can see it is simply applying a translation, calling the simple scale method, and applying the opposite translation:

```
    public final void scale(float sx, float sy, float px, float py) {
        translate(px, py);
        scale(sx, sy);
        translate(-px, -py);
    }
```

Using this method, we could have implemented the `onDraw()` method this other way:

```
    @Override
    protected void onDraw(Canvas canvas) {
        float angle = (System.currentTimeMillis() - timeStart) / 100.f;

        canvas.drawColor(BACKGROUND_COLOR);

        canvas.save();
        canvas.translate(canvas.getWidth() / 2,
                        canvas.getHeight() / 2);

        for (int i = 0; i < 15; i++) {
```

```
        canvas.rotate(angle, rectSize / 2, rectSize / 2);
        canvas.drawRect(0, 0, rectSize, rectSize, paint);
        canvas.scale(1.2f, 1.2f, rectSize / 2, rectSize / 2);
    }

    canvas.restore();
    invalidate();
}
```

See the following screenshot to see how the rectangles are concatenated:

In addition, the source code of this full example can be found in the Example21-Transformations folder on the GitHub repository.

We've seen some basic operations on matrices, such as `scale()`, `rotate()`, and `translate()`, but `canvas` provides us with some more additional methods:

- `skew`: This applies a skew transformation.
- `setMatrix`: This lets us compute a transformation matrix and directly sets it to our `canvas`.
- `concat`: This is similar to the previous case. We can concatenate any matrix to the current one.

Putting it all together

So far, we've seen many different drawing primitives, clipping operations, and matrix transformations, but the most interesting part is when we combine it all together. In order to build great custom views, we've to use many different kinds of operations and transformations.

However, having so many operations available is a double-edged sword. We have to be careful when adding this complexity to our custom view, as we can compromise performance quite easily. We should check if we're applying, for example, too many or unnecessary clippings operations or if we aren't optimizing enough or we aren't maximizing reuse of clipping and transformation operations. In that case, we might even use the `quickReject()` method from the `canvas` object to quickly discard areas that will fall outside the clipping area.

Also, we need to keep track of all `save()` and `restore()` we're performing to our `canvas`. Performing additional `restore()` methods, not only means we have an issue with our code, but is an actual error. If we have to change to different previously saved states, we can use the `restoreToCount()` method together with saving the state number in the call we do to save the state.

As we've mentioned before, and will mention again in the following chapters, avoid to allocate memory or create new instances of an object, inside the `onDraw()` method; especially remember this remark if at some point you think you have to create a new instance of a `paint` object inside the `onDraw()`. Reuse `paint` objects or initialize them, for instance, on the class constructor.

Summary

In this chapter, we've seen how to draw more complex graphic primitives, transform them, and use clipping operations while drawing our custom view. Most of the time, these primitives by themselves don't give us too much value but, we've also saw many quick examples of how to put many of them together and create something useful. We didn't cover all the possible methods, operations, or transformations, as it will be a lot of information and will not be useful; it may seem like reading a language dictionary. To stay up to date with all the possible methods and drawing primitives, keep checking the developer's Android documentation and stay aware of the release notes of every new release of Android to check what's new.

In the next chapter, we'll see how to use OpenGL ES to add 3D rendering to our custom view.

5
Introducing 3D Custom Views

In previous chapters, we've seen how to implement custom views using the Android 2D graphics library. That would be our most common approach, but sometimes, we might need some more horsepower because of additional render particularities or the requirements of our custom view. In those cases, we might use **OpenGL for Embedded Systems** (**OpenGL ES**) and enable 3D rendering operations in our view.

In this chapter, we'll see how to use OpenGL ES in our custom views and show a practical example of how we can build one. With more detail, we will cover the following topics:

- Introduction to OpenGL ES
- Drawing geometry
- Loading external geometry

Introduction to OpenGL ES

Android supports OpenGL ES for 3D rendering. OpenGL ES is a subset of the desktop **OpenGL API** implementation. On its own, **Open Graphics Library** (**OpenGL**) is a very popular cross-platform API for rendering 2D and 3D graphics.

It is slightly more complex to use OpenGL ES to render our custom view than the standard Android canvas drawing primitives and, as we'll see during this chapter, it needs to be used with common sense and it won't always be the best approach.

For any additional information about OpenGL ES please refer to the official documentation from The Khronos Group:
`https://www.khronos.org/opengles/`.

Getting started with OpenGL ES in Android

It's very easy to create a 3D-enabled custom view. We can do it by simply extending `GLSurfaceView` instead of just extending from the `View` class. The complexity comes in the rendering part, but let's go step by step. First, we'll create a class named `GLDrawer` and add it to our project:

```
package com.packt.rrafols.draw;

import android.content.Context;
import android.opengl.GLSurfaceView;
import android.util.AttributeSet;

public class GLDrawer extends GLSurfaceView {
    private GLRenderer glRenderer;

    public GLDrawer(Context context, AttributeSet attributeSet) {
        super(context, attributeSet);
    }
}
```

Like our previous examples, we created the constructor with the `AttributeSet`, so we can inflate it and set parameters, if needed, from the XML layout file.

We might have the impression that OpenGL ES is only used in full screen games, but it can be used in non-full screen views and even inside `ViewGroups` or a `ScrollView`.

To see how it behaves, let's add it to the `layout` file between two `TextView`:

```
<?xml version="1.0" encoding="utf-8"?>
<LinearLayout
    xmlns:android="http://schemas.android.com/apk/res/android"
    xmlns:tools="http://schemas.android.com/tools"
    android:id="@+id/activity_main"
    android:layout_width="match_parent"
    android:layout_height="match_parent"
    android:orientation="vertical"
    android:padding="@dimen/activity_vertical_margin"
    tools:context="com.packt.rrafols.draw.MainActivity">

<TextView
```

```
        android:layout_width="match_parent"
        android:layout_height="100dp"
        android:background="@android:color/background_light"
        android:gravity="center_vertical|center_horizontal"
        android:text="@string/filler_text"/>

    <com.packt.rrafols.draw.GLDrawer
        android:layout_width="match_parent"
        android:layout_height="100dp"/>

    <TextView
        android:layout_width="match_parent"
        android:layout_height="100dp"
        android:background="@android:color/background_light"
        android:gravity="center_vertical|center_horizontal"
        android:text="@string/filler_text"/>
</LinearLayout>
```

We need to do an additional step before our GLDrawer class can work. We have to create a
GLSurfaceView.Renderer object to handle all the rendering and set it to the view by
using the setRenderer() method. When we set this renderer, GLSurfaceView will
additionally create a new thread to manage the drawing cycle of the view. Let's add a
GLRenderer class at the end of the GLDrawer class file:

```
class GLRenderer implements GLSurfaceView.Renderer {
    @Override
    public void onSurfaceCreated(GL10 gl, EGLConfig config) {

    }

    @Override
    public void onSurfaceChanged(GL10 gl, int width, int height) {

    }

    @Override
    public void onDrawFrame(GL10 gl) {
        gl.glClearColor(1.f, 0.f, 0.f, 1.f);
        gl.glClear(GL10.GL_COLOR_BUFFER_BIT);
    }
}
```

The `glClearColor()` method tells OpenGL which color we'd like to clear from the screen. We're setting the four components, red, green, blue, and alpha, in a floating-point format ranging from 0 to 1. `glClear()` is the method that actually clears the screen. As OpenGL can also clear several other buffers, it'll only clear the screen if we set the `GL_COLOR_BUFFER_BIT` flag. Now that we've been introduced to some OpenGL functions, let's create a `GLRenderer` instance variable and initialize it in the class constructor:

```
private GLRenderer glRenderer;
public GLDrawer(Context context, AttributeSet attributeSet) {
    super(context, attributeSet);
    glRenderer = new GLRenderer()
    setRenderer(glRenderer);
}
```

When implementing a `GLSurfaceView.Renderer` class, we have to override the following three methods or callbacks:

- `onSurfaceCreated()`: This method will be called every time Android needs to create an OpenGL context-for example, the very first time the rendered thread is created, or every time the OpenGL context is lost. Context might be lost whenever the application goes into the background. This callback is the ideal method to put all the initialization code that depends on the OpenGL context.
- `onSurfaceChanged()`: This method will be called when the view is resized. It'll also be called the very first time the surface is created.
- `onDrawFrame()`: This method is responsible for doing the actual drawing, and will be called every time the view needs to be drawn.

In our example, we've left the `onSurfaceCreated()` and `onSurfaceChanged()` methods empty as, at this moment, we're only focusing on drawing a solid background to check if we have everything working, and we don't need the view size yet.

If we run this example, we'll see both `TextViews` and our custom view with a red background:

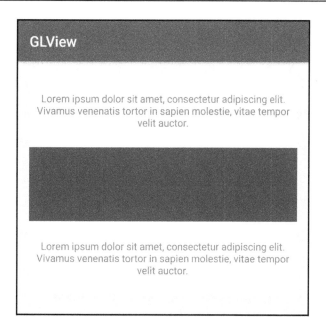

If we set a breakpoint or we print a log in our `onDrawFrame()` method, we'll see that the view is continuously redrawn. This behavior is different from a normal view, as the renderer thread will be continuously calling the `onDrawFrame()` method. This behavior can be modified by calling the `setRender()` method once we've set the renderer object. If we call it before, it'll crash our application. There are two render modes:

- `setRenderMode(RENDERMODE_CONTINUOUSLY)`: This is the default behavior. The renderer will be continuously called to render the view.
- `setRenderMode(RENDERMODE_WHEN_DIRTY)`: This can be set to avoid the continuous redrawing of the view. Instead of calling invalidate, we have to call `requestRender` in order to request a new render of the view.

Drawing basic geometry

We've got our view initialized and have drawn a solid red background. Let's draw something more interesting. We'll focus on OpenGL ES 2.0 in the following examples, as it's been available since Android 2.2, or API level 8, and it's not really worth explaining how to do it in OpenGL ES 1.1. However, if you want to know more, there are some ports of the old NeHe OpenGL ES tutorials ported to Android on GitHub:
`https://github.com/nea/nehe-android-ports`.

OpenGLES 1.1 and OpenGL ES 2.0 code are incompatible because the OpenGL ES 1.1 code is based on a fixed-function pipeline, where you have to specify the geometry, lights, and so on, and OpenGL ES 2.0 is based on a programmable pipeline handled by the vertex and fragment shaders.

First, as we require OpenGL ES 2.0, we should add a `uses-feature` configuration line in our manifest file so that Google Play will not show the application to those devices that are not compatible:

```
<application>
    ....
<uses-feature android:glEsVersion="0x00020000" android:required="true" />
    ...
</application>
```

If we use specific APIs from OpenGL ES3.0, we'd change the requirement to `android:glEsVersion="0x00030000"` to let Google Play filter accordingly.

Once we've done this step, we could start drawing some more shapes and geometry. But first, before setting the renderer, we should set the renderer context to 2 so it will create an OpenGL ES 2.0 context. We can easily do that by modifying the constructor of the `GLDrawer` class:

```
public GLDrawer(Context context, AttributeSet attributeSet) {
    super(context, attributeSet);
    setEGLContextClientVersion(2);
    glRenderer = new GLRenderer();
    setRenderer(glRenderer);
}
```

Let's now go through how to draw a rectangle on the screen, step by step. If you're familiar with OpenGL ES 1.1 but not with OpenGL ES 2.0, you'll see that there is a bit more work to do, but at the end, we'll benefit from the additional flexibility and power of OpenGL ES 2.0.

We will start by defining an array with the coordinates of a rectangle, or a quad, centered on the position 0, 0, 0:

```
private float quadCoords[] = {
    -1.f, -1.f, 0.0f,
    -1.f,  1.f, 0.0f,
     1.f,  1.f, 0.0f,
     1.f, -1.f, 0.0f
};
```

We'll be drawing triangles, so we have to define their vertex indexes:

```
private short[] index = {
    0, 1, 2,
    0, 2, 3
};
```

To understand the reasoning behind these indexes, how to map them to the vertex indexes we previously defined, and how we can draw a quad using two triangles, look at the following diagram:

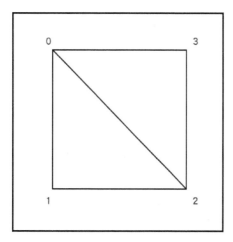

If we draw a triangle with the vertices 0, 1, and 2, and another one with the vertices 0, 2, and 3, we'll end up having a quad.

When working with OpenGL ES, we'll need to provide data using a `Buffer` or a subclass of a `Buffer`, so let's convert those arrays into `Buffer`:

```
ByteBuffer vbb = ByteBuffer.allocateDirect(quadCoords.length * (Float.SIZE
/ 8));
vbb.order(ByteOrder.nativeOrder());

vertexBuffer = vbb.asFloatBuffer();
vertexBuffer.put(quadCoords);
vertexBuffer.position(0);
```

First, we have to allocate the space we need for the `Buffer`. As we know the size of the array, this would be very easy: We just have to multiply it by the size of a float in bytes. One float is exactly four bytes, but we can calculate it by getting the number of bits using `Float.SIZE` and dividing it by 8. In Java 8, there is a new constant called `Float.BYTES` that precisely returns the size in bytes.

We have to indicate that the `Buffer` in which we put the data will have the native byte order of the platform. We can do this by calling the `order()` method on the `Buffer` with `ByteOrder.nativeOrder()` as a parameter. Once we've done this step, we can convert it to a float buffer by calling `Buffer.asFloatBuffer()` and set the data. To finish, we reset the position of the `Buffer` to the beginning by setting its position to 0.

We have to do this process for the vertices as well as for the indexes. As indexes are stored as short integers, we need to take that into consideration when we convert the buffer, and when calculating the size:

```
ByteBuffer ibb = ByteBuffer.allocateDirect(index.length * (Short.SIZE /
8));
ibb.order(ByteOrder.nativeOrder());

indexBuffer = ibb.asShortBuffer();
indexBuffer.put(index);
indexBuffer.position(0);
```

As we mentioned before, the OpenGL ES 2.0 rendering pipeline is handled by the vertex and the fragment `shader`. Let's create a helper method to load and compile the `shader` code:

```
// Source:
// https://developer.android.com/training/graphics/opengl/draw.html
public static int loadShader(int type, String shaderCode){

    // create a vertex shader type (GLES20.GL_VERTEX_SHADER)
    // or a fragment shader type (GLES20.GL_FRAGMENT_SHADER)
    int shader = GLES20.glCreateShader(type);

    // add the source code to the shader and compile it
    GLES20.glShaderSource(shader, shaderCode);
    GLES20.glCompileShader(shader);

    return shader;
}
```

Using this new method, we can load both the vertex and fragment `shaders`:

```
private void initShaders() {
    int vertexShader = loadShader(GLES20.GL_VERTEX_SHADER,
vertexShaderCode);
    int fragmentShader = loadShader(GLES20.GL_FRAGMENT_SHADER,
fragmentShaderCode);

    shaderProgram = GLES20.glCreateProgram();
    GLES20.glAttachShader(shaderProgram, vertexShader);
    GLES20.glAttachShader(shaderProgram, fragmentShader);
    GLES20.glLinkProgram(shaderProgram);
}
```

For the time being, let's use the default `shaders` from the Android developer's OpenGL training website.

The `vertexShader` is as follows:

```
// Source:
// https://developer.android.com/training/graphics/opengl/draw.html
private final String vertexShaderCode =
        // This matrix member variable provides a hook to manipulate
        // the coordinates of the objects that use this vertex shader
"uniform mat4 uMVPMatrix;" +
"attribute vec4 vPosition;" +
"void main() {" +
        // The matrix must be included as a modifier of gl_Position.
        // Note that the uMVPMatrix factor *must be first* in order
        // for the matrix multiplication product to be correct.
"  gl_Position = uMVPMatrix * vPosition;" +
"}";
```

The `fragmentShader` is as follows:

```
private final String fragmentShaderCode =
"precision mediump float;" +
"uniform vec4 vColor;" +
"void main() {" +
"  gl_FragColor = vColor;" +
"}";
```

We've added a matrix multiplication in our `vertexShader`, so we can modify the position of the vertices by updating the `uMVPMatrix`. Let's add a projection and some transformations in order to have the basic rendering in place.

We shouldn't forget about the `onSurfaceChanged()` callback; let's use it to set our projection matrix and define the clipping planes of our camera, taking into account the width and height of the screen to keep its aspect ratio:

```
@Override
public void onSurfaceChanged(GL10 unused, int width, int height) {
    GLES20.glViewport(0, 0, width, height);

    float ratio = (float) width / height;
    Matrix.frustumM(mProjectionMatrix, 0, -ratio * 2, ratio * 2, -2, 2,
    3, 7);
}
```

Let's compute the view matrix by using `Matrix.setLookAtM()` and multiplying it by the projection matrix we've just calculated on `mProjectionMatrix`:

```
@Override
public void onDrawFrame(GL10 unused) {

    ...

    Matrix.multiplyMM(mMVPMatrix, 0, mProjectionMatrix, 0, mViewMatrix,
    0);

    int mMVPMatrixHandle = GLES20.glGetUniformLocation(shaderProgram,
    "uMVPMatrix");
    GLES20.glUniformMatrix4fv(mMVPMatrixHandle, 1, false, mMVPMatrix,
    0);

    ...

}
```

In the preceding code, we also saw how to update a variable that can be read from a `shader`. To do so, we need to get the handle of the uniform variable first. By using `GLES20.glGetUniformLocation(shaderProgram, "uMVPMatrix")` we can get the handle of the `uMVPMatrix` uniform variable and, using this handle on the `GLES20.glUniformMatrix4fv` call, we can set the matrix we've just calculated onto it. If we check the code for the `shader`, we can see we've defined `uMVPMatrix` as uniform:

```
uniform mat4 uMVPMatrix;
```

Now that we know how to set a uniform variable, let's do the same with the color. On the fragment `shader`, we've set `vColor` as a uniform variable as well, so we can follow the same method to set it:

```
float color[] = { 0.2f, 0.2f, 0.9f, 1.0f };

...

int colorHandle = GLES20.glGetUniformLocation(shaderProgram, "vColor");
GLES20.glUniform4fv(colorHandle, 1, color, 0);
```

Using the same mechanism, but changing `glGetUniformLocation` to `glGetAttribLocation`, we can also set the vertex coordinates:

```
int positionHandle = GLES20.glGetAttribLocation(shaderProgram,
    "vPosition");

GLES20.glVertexAttribPointer(positionHandle, 3,
        GLES20.GL_FLOAT, false,
        3 * 4, vertexBuffer);
```

We have everything ready to draw it to the screen; we just have to enable the vertex attribute array, as we've set the coordinate data using the `glVertexAttribPointer()` call and `glDrawElements()` will only draw enabled arrays:

```
GLES20.glEnableVertexAttribArray(positionHandle);

GLES20.glDrawElements(
        GLES20.GL_TRIANGLES, index.length,
        GLES20.GL_UNSIGNED_SHORT, indexBuffer);

GLES20.glDisableVertexAttribArray(positionHandle);
```

There are many mays of drawing geometry on OpenGL, but we've used the `glDrawElements()` call pointing to the buffer of the face indexes we've previously created. We've used `GL_TRIANGLES` primitive here, but there are many other OpenGL primitives we can use. Check the official Khronos documentation about `glDrawElements()` for more information:

`https://www.khronos.org/registry/OpenGL-Refpages/gl4/html/glDrawElements.xhtml`.

Also, as good practice, and to restore the OpenGL machine state, we disable the vertex attribute array after drawing.

If we execute this code, we'll get the following-still not really useful, but it's a start!

Check the `Example23-GLSurfaceView` in the GitHub repository for the full example source code.

Drawing geometry

So far, we've seen how to set up our OpenGL renderer and draw some very basic geometry. But, as you can imagine, we can do a lot more with OpenGL. In this section we'll see how to do some more complex operations and how to load geometry defined using an external tool. Sometimes, it might come in useful to define the geometry using code, but most of the time, and especially if the geometry is very complex, it'll be designed and created using a 3D modeling tool. Knowing how we can import that geometry will definitely come in very handy for our projects.

Adding volume

In our previous example, we've seen how to draw a quad with one single color, but what about if each vertex has a completely different color? The process will not be very different from what we've already done, but let's see how we can do it.

First, let's change the color array to hold the color of the four vertices:

```
float color[] = {
        1.0f, 0.2f, 0.2f, 1.0f,
        0.2f, 1.0f, 0.2f, 1.0f,
        0.2f, 0.2f, 1.0f, 1.0f,
        1.0f, 1.0f, 1.0f, 1.0f,
};
```

Now, in our `initBuffers()` method, let's initialize an additional `Buffer` for the color:

```
private FloatBuffer colorBuffer;

...

ByteBuffer cbb = ByteBuffer.allocateDirect(color.length * (Float.SIZE /
8));
cbb.order(ByteOrder.nativeOrder());

colorBuffer = cbb.asFloatBuffer();
colorBuffer.put(color);
colorBuffer.position(0);
```

We have to update our `shaders` as well to take the color parameter into account. First, on our `vertexShader`, we have to create a new attribute that we will call `aColor` to hold the color of each vertex:

```
private final String vertexShaderCode =
"uniform mat4 uMVPMatrix;" +
"attribute vec4 vPosition;" +
"attribute vec4 aColor;" +
"varying vec4 vColor;" +
"void main() {" +
"  gl_Position = uMVPMatrix * vPosition;" +
"  vColor = aColor;" +
"}";
```

Then, we define a varying vColor variable that will be passed to the fragmentShader, and the fragmentShader will compute the value per fragment. Let's see the changes on the fragmentShader:

```
private final String fragmentShaderCode =
"precision mediump float;" +
"varying vec4 vColor;" +
"void main() {" +
"  gl_FragColor = vColor;" +
"}";
```

The only thing we've changed is the declaration of vColor; instead of being a uniform variable, now it's a varying variable.

Just like we did with the vertex and face indexes, we have to set the color data to the shader:

```
int colorHandle = GLES20.glGetAttribLocation(shaderProgram, "aColor");
GLES20.glVertexAttribPointer(colorHandle, 4,
        GLES20.GL_FLOAT, false,
        4 * 4, colorBuffer);
```

Before drawing, we have to enable and disable the vertex array. If the color array is not enabled, we'll get a black square instead, as glDrawElements() will not be able to get the color information;

```
GLES20.glEnableVertexAttribArray(colorHandle);
GLES20.glEnableVertexAttribArray(positionHandle);
GLES20.glDrawElements(
        GLES20.GL_TRIANGLES, index.length,
        GLES20.GL_UNSIGNED_SHORT, indexBuffer);

GLES20.glDisableVertexAttribArray(positionHandle);
GLES20.glDisableVertexAttribArray(colorHandle);
```

If we run this example, we'll see a similar effect as our previous example, but we can see how the color is interpolated between the vertices:

Now that we know how to interpolate colors, let's add some depth into the geometry. Everything we've drawn so far is quite flat, so let's convert the quad into a cube. It is very straightforward. Lets first define the vertices and new face indexes:

```java
private float quadCoords[] = {
        -1.f, -1.f, -1.0f,
        -1.f,  1.f, -1.0f,
         1.f,  1.f, -1.0f,
         1.f, -1.f, -1.0f,

        -1.f, -1.f,  1.0f,
        -1.f,  1.f,  1.0f,
         1.f,  1.f,  1.0f,
         1.f, -1.f,  1.0f
};
```

We've replicated the same four vertices we had before, but with a displaced Z coordinate, that would add volume to the cube.

Now, we have to create the new face indexes. A cube has six faces, or quads, that can be reproduced with twelve triangles:

```
private short[] index = {
        0, 1, 2,          // front
        0, 2, 3,          // front
        4, 5, 6,          // back
        4, 6, 7,          // back
        0, 4, 7,          // top
        0, 3, 7,          // top
        1, 5, 6,          // bottom
        1, 2, 6,          // bottom
        0, 4, 5,          // left
        0, 1, 5,          // left
        3, 7, 6,          // right
        3, 2, 6           // right
};
```

Lets also add new colors for the new four vertices:

```
float color[] = {
        1.0f, 0.2f, 0.2f, 1.0f,
        0.2f, 1.0f, 0.2f, 1.0f,
        0.2f, 0.2f, 1.0f, 1.0f,
        1.0f, 1.0f, 1.0f, 1.0f,

        1.0f, 1.0f, 0.2f, 1.0f,
        0.2f, 1.0f, 1.0f, 1.0f,
        1.0f, 0.2f, 1.0f, 1.0f,
        0.2f, 0.2f, 0.2f, 1.0f
};
```

If we execute this example, as it is, we'll get a strange result, similar to the following screenshot:

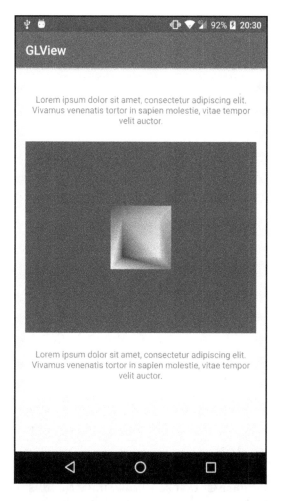

Lets add a rotation transformation to the mMVPMatrix matrix to see what is going on.

We have to define a private variable to hold the rotation angle and apply the rotation to the mMVPMatrix:

```
private float angle = 0.f;
...
Matrix.setLookAtM(mViewMatrix, 0,
        0, 0, -4,
        0f, 0f, 0f,
        0f, 1.0f, 0.0f);

Matrix.multiplyMM(mMVPMatrix, 0, mProjectionMatrix, 0, mViewMatrix, 0);
Matrix.rotateM(mMVPMatrix, 0, angle, 1.f, 1.f, 1.f);
```

In this case, just to see what is going on, we're applying the rotation to the three axes: *x*, *y*, and *z*. We also moved the camera a bit away from our previous example, as now there might be some clipping if we don't do so.

To define the amount we have to rotate by, we'll use one of the Android timers:

```
private long startTime;
...
@Override
public void onSurfaceCreated(GL10 unused, EGLConfig config) {
    initBuffers();
    initShaders();
    startTime = SystemClock.elapsedRealtime();
}
```

We store the start time on the startTime variable, and on our onDrawFrame() method we compute the angle based on the amount of time that has passed since this moment:

```
angle = ((float) SystemClock.elapsedRealtime() - startTime) * 0.02f;
```

Here, we have just multiplied it by 0.02f to limit the speed of rotation, as otherwise it'll be too fast. Doing it this way, the animation speed will be the same on all devices regardless of the rendering frame rate or their CPU speed. Now, if we run this code, we'll see the origin of the issue we're experiencing:

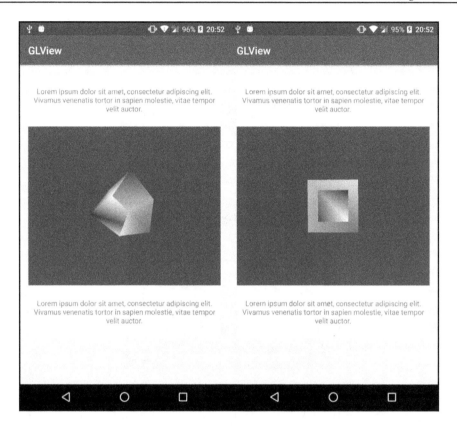

The issue is that OpenGL is not checking the z coordinate of the pixel when drawing all the triangles, so there might be some superposition and overdrawing as we can easily see in the preceding screenshots. Luckily for us, this is very easy to solve. OpenGL has a state that we can use to enable and disable depth, or z, tests:

```
GLES20.glEnable(GLES20.GL_DEPTH_TEST);
GLES20.glEnableVertexAttribArray(colorHandle);
GLES20.glEnableVertexAttribArray(positionHandle);
GLES20.glDrawElements(
        GLES20.GL_TRIANGLES, index.length,
        GLES20.GL_UNSIGNED_SHORT, indexBuffer);

GLES20.glDisableVertexAttribArray(positionHandle);
GLES20.glDisableVertexAttribArray(colorHandle);
GLES20.glDisable(GLES20.GL_DEPTH_TEST);
```

As with the previous example, after drawing we disable the state we've enabled to avoid leaving an unknown OpenGL state for any other drawing operation. If we run this code, we'll see the difference:

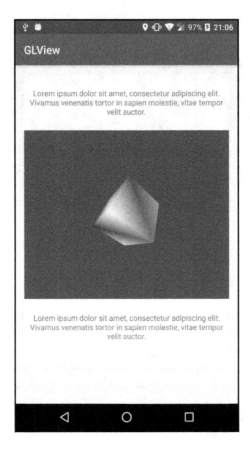

Check the `Example24-GLDrawing` on the GitHub repository for the full example source code.

Adding textures

Let's keep doing more interesting things! We've seen how to add a color per vertex, but let's see now what do we have to change if we want to add some textures to our 3D object.

First, let's replace the color array with a texture coordinate array. We'll map texture coordinate 0 to the start of our texture, in both axes, and 1 to the end of the texture, also in both axes. Using the geometry we had in our previous example, we could then define the texture coordinates this way:

```
private float texCoords[] = {
        1.f, 1.f,
        1.f, 0.f,
        0.f, 0.f,
        0.f, 1.f,

        1.f, 1.f,
        1.f, 0.f,
        0.f, 0.f,
        0.f, 1.f,
};
```

To load these texture coordinates, we use exactly the same procedure as we did previously:

```
ByteBuffer tbb = ByteBuffer.allocateDirect(texCoords.length * (Float.SIZE /
8));
tbb.order(ByteOrder.nativeOrder());

texBuffer = tbb.asFloatBuffer();
texBuffer.put(texCoords);
texBuffer.position(0);
```

Let's also create a helper method to load a resource into a texture:

```
private int loadTexture(int resId) {
    final int[] textureIds = new int[1];
    GLES20.glGenTextures(1, textureIds, 0);

    if (textureIds[0] == 0) return -1;

    // do not scale the bitmap depending on screen density
    final BitmapFactory.Options options = new BitmapFactory.Options();
    options.inScaled = false;

    final Bitmap textureBitmap =
    BitmapFactory.decodeResource(getResources(), resId, options);
    GLES20.glBindTexture(GLES20.GL_TEXTURE_2D, textureIds[0]);
```

```
GLES20.glTexParameteri(GLES20.GL_TEXTURE_2D,
        GLES20.GL_TEXTURE_MIN_FILTER, GLES20.GL_NEAREST);

GLES20.glTexParameteri(GLES20.GL_TEXTURE_2D,
        GLES20.GL_TEXTURE_MAG_FILTER, GLES20.GL_NEAREST);

GLES20.glTexParameterf(GLES20.GL_TEXTURE_2D,
        GLES20.GL_TEXTURE_WRAP_S, GLES20.GL_CLAMP_TO_EDGE);

GLES20.glTexParameterf(GLES20.GL_TEXTURE_2D,
        GLES20.GL_TEXTURE_WRAP_T, GLES20.GL_CLAMP_TO_EDGE);

GLUtils.texImage2D(GLES20.GL_TEXTURE_2D, 0, textureBitmap, 0);
textureBitmap.recycle();

return textureIds[0];
}
```

We have to take into account that both texture dimensions have to be to the power of 2. To preserve the original size of the image and avoid any scaling done by Android, we have to set the bitmap options `inScaled` flag to `false`. In the previous code, we generate a texture ID to hold the reference to our texture, binding it as the active texture, setting the parameters of filtering and wrapping, and finally loading the bitmap data. Once we've done so, we can recycle the temporary bitmap, as we don't need it anymore.

As we did before, we have to update our `shaders` as well. In our `vertexShader`, we have to apply almost the same changes as we did before, adding an attribute where we can set the vertex texture coordinate and a `varying` variable to pass to the `fragmentShader`:

```
private final String vertexShaderCode =
"uniform mat4 uMVPMatrix;" +
"attribute vec4 vPosition;" +
"attribute vec2 aTex;" +
"varying vec2 vTex;" +
"void main() {" +
"   gl_Position = uMVPMatrix * vPosition;" +
"   vTex = aTex;" +
"}";
```

Note that the vertex coordinates are a vec2 instead of a vec4, as we only have two coordinates: U and V. Our new `fragmentShader` is a bit more complex than the one we had before:

```
private final String fragmentShaderCode =
"precision mediump float;" +
"uniform sampler2D sTex;" +
"varying vec2 vTex;" +
```

```
"void main() {" +
"  gl_FragColor = texture2D(sTex, vTex);" +
"}";
```

We have to create the `varying` texture coordinate variable and also a uniform `sampler2D` variable where we'll set the active texture. To get the color, we have to use the `texture2D` lookup function to read the color data from the texture on the specified coordinates.

Let's now add a bitmap named `texture.png` to our drawables `res` folder and modify the `onSurfaceCreated()` method to load it as a texture:

```
@Override
public void onSurfaceCreated(GL10 unused, EGLConfig config) {
    initBuffers();
    initShaders();

    textureId = loadTexture(R.drawable.texture);

    startTime = SystemClock.elapsedRealtime();
}
```

Here is the image used in our example:

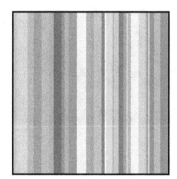

Finally, let's update the `onDrawFrame()` method to set the texture coordinates:

```
int texCoordHandle = GLES20.glGetAttribLocation(shaderProgram, "aTex");
GLES20.glVertexAttribPointer(texCoordHandle, 2,
        GLES20.GL_FLOAT, false,
        0, texBuffer);
```

Here is the texture itself:

```
int texHandle = GLES20.glGetUniformLocation(shaderProgram, "sTex");
GLES20.glActiveTexture(GLES20.GL_TEXTURE0);
GLES20.glBindTexture(GLES20.GL_TEXTURE_2D, textureId);
GLES20.glUniform1i(texHandle, 0);
```

Also, as we did before, we have to enable, and later disable, the texture coordinates vertex array.

If we run this code, we'll get the following:

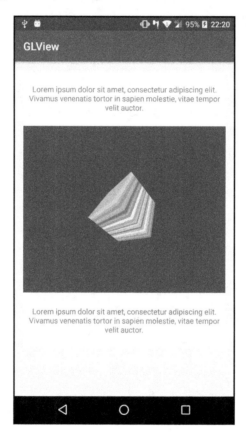

Check the `Example25-GLDrawing` on the GitHub repository for the full example source code.

Loading external geometry

So far, we've been drawing quads and cubes, but if we want to draw more complex geometry, it is probably handier to model it on a 3D modeling tool rather than doing it by code. We can cover multiple chapters on this topic, but let's just look at a quick example of how can it be done and you can extend it to your needs.

We have used a Blender to model our example data. Blender is a free and open source 3D modeling toolset and can be downloaded for free at its website:
`https://www.blender.org/`.

For this example, we haven't modeled an extremely complex example; we've just used one of the primitives that Blender provides: Suzanne:

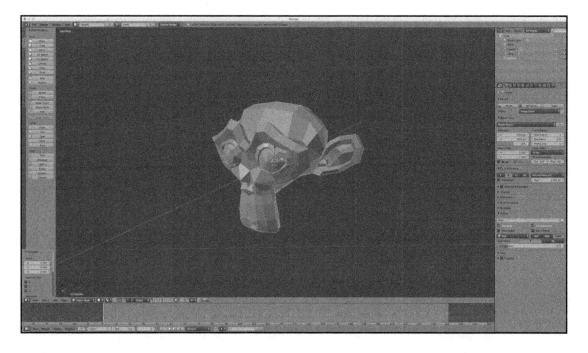

To simplify our importing tool, we'll select the object mesh under the **Scene | Suzanne** drop-down menu on the right and, when we press *Ctrl + T*, Blender will convert all faces into triangles. Otherwise, we'll have both triangles and quads on our exported file and it's not straightforward to implement the face importer from our Android application code:

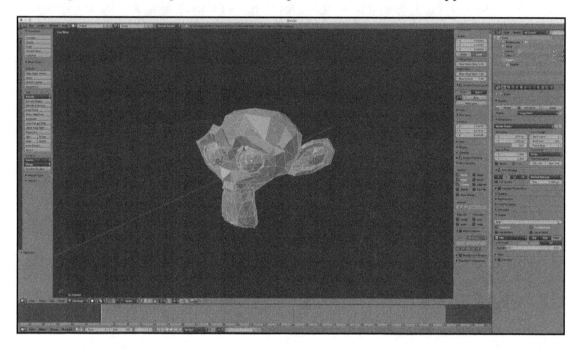

Now, we'll export it as a `Wavefront` (`.obj`) file, which will create both a `.obj` and a `.mtl` file. The latter is the material information that, for the moment, we'll ignore. Let's put the exported file into our project in the `assets` folder.

Let's now create a very simple `Wavefront` file object parser ourselves. As we'll be dealing with files, loading, and parsing, we'll have to do it asynchronously:

```
public class WavefrontObjParser {
    public static void parse(Context context, String name, ParserListener
listener) {
        WavefrontObjParserHelper helper = new
WavefrontObjParserHelper(context, name, listener);
        helper.start();
    }

    public interface ParserListener {
        void parsingSuccess(Scene scene);
```

```
        void parsingError(String message);
    }
}
```

As you can see, there is no actual work done here. To do the real loading and parsing, we've created a helper class that will do it on a separate **thread** and call the listener either if it's successful or if there has been an error parsing the file:

```
class WavefrontObjParserHelper extends Thread {
    private String name;
    private WavefrontObjParser.ParserListener listener;
    private Context context;

    WavefrontObjParserHelper(Context context, String name,
    WavefrontObjParser.ParserListener listener) {
        this.context = context;
        this.name = name;
        this.listener = listener;
    }
}
```

Then, when we call `helper.start()`, it'll create the actual thread, and execute the `run()` method on it:

```
public void run() {
        try {

            InputStream is = context.getAssets().open(name);
            BufferedReader br = new BufferedReader(new
            InputStreamReader(is));

            Scene scene = new Scene();
            Object3D obj = null;

            String str;
            while ((str = br.readLine()) != null) {
                if (!str.startsWith("#")) {
                    String[] line = str.split("");

                    if("o".equals(line[0])) {
                        if (obj != null) obj.prepare();
                        obj = new Object3D();
                        scene.addObject(obj);

                    } else if("v".equals(line[0])) {
                        float x = Float.parseFloat(line[1]);
                        float y = Float.parseFloat(line[2]);
                        float z = Float.parseFloat(line[3]);
                        obj.addCoordinate(x, y, z);
```

```
            } else if("f".equals(line[0])) {

                int a = getFaceIndex(line[1]);
                int b = getFaceIndex(line[2]);
                int c = getFaceIndex(line[3]);

                if (line.length == 4) {
                    obj.addFace(a, b, c);
                } else {
                    int d = getFaceIndex(line[4]);
                    obj.addFace(a, b, c, d);
                }
            } else {
                // skip
            }
        }
    }
    if (obj != null) obj.prepare();
    br.close();

    if (listener != null) listener.parsingSuccess(scene);
} catch(Exception e) {
    if (listener != null) listener.parsingError(e.getMessage());
    e.printStackTrace();
}
}
```

In the previous code, we first read the asset by opening the file with the name provided. To get the application assets, we need a context here:

```
InputStream is = context.getAssets().open(name);
BufferedReader br = new BufferedReader(new InputStreamReader(is));
```

Then, we read the file line by line and we take different actions depending on the starting keyword, except if the line starts with #, which means that it's a comment. We're only taking into consideration the commands of a new object, vertex coordinates, and face index; we're ignoring any additional commands that there might be on the file, such as material used, or vertex and face normals.

As we can get face index information, such as **f 330//278 336//278 338//278 332//278**, we created a helper method to parse that information and only extract the face index. The number after the slashes is the face normal index. Refer to the official file format to understand the usage of the face index numbers in more detail:

```
private static int getFaceIndex(String face) {
    if(!face.contains("/")) {
        return Integer.parseInt(face) - 1;
```

```
        } else {
            return Integer.parseInt(face.split("/")[0]) - 1;
        }
    }
```

Also, as face indices start at 1, we have to subtract 1 to get it right.

To store all this data we're reading from the file, we've also created some data classes. The Object3D class will store all relevant information-vertices, face indexes, and the Scene class will store the whole 3D scene with all the Objects3D inside. For simplicity, we've kept these implementations as short as possible, but they can be made way more complex depending on our needs:

```
public class Scene {
    private ArrayList<Object3D> objects;

    public Scene() {
        objects = new ArrayList<>();
    }

    public void addObject(Object3D obj) {
        objects.add(obj);
    }

    public ArrayList<Object3D> getObjects() {
        return objects;
    }

    public void render(int shaderProgram, String posAttributeName,
    String colAttributeName) {
        GLES20.glEnable(GLES20.GL_DEPTH_TEST);

        for (int i = 0; i < objects.size(); i++) {
            objects.get(i).render(shaderProgram, posAttributeName,
            colAttributeName);
        }

        GLES20.glDisable(GLES20.GL_DEPTH_TEST);
    }
}
```

We can see that there is a `render()` method on the `Scene` class. We've moved the responsibility of rendering all its 3D objects to the `Scene` itself, and, applying the same principle, each object is also responsible for rendering itself:

```
public void prepare() {
    if (coordinateList.size() > 0 && coordinates == null) {
        coordinates = new float[coordinateList.size()];
        for (int i = 0; i < coordinateList.size(); i++) {
            coordinates[i] = coordinateList.get(i);
        }
    }

    if (indexList.size() > 0 && indexes == null) {
        indexes = new short[indexList.size()];
        for (int i = 0; i < indexList.size(); i++) {
            indexes[i] = indexList.get(i);
        }
    }

    colors = new float[(coordinates.length/3) * 4];
    for (int i = 0; i < colors.length/4; i++) {
        float intensity = (float) (Math.random() * 0.5 + 0.4);
        colors[i * 4    ] = intensity;
        colors[i * 4 + 1] = intensity;
        colors[i * 4 + 2] = intensity;
        colors[i * 4 + 3] = 1.f;
    }

    ByteBuffer vbb = ByteBuffer.allocateDirect(coordinates.length *
    (Float.SIZE / 8));
    vbb.order(ByteOrder.nativeOrder());

    vertexBuffer = vbb.asFloatBuffer();
    vertexBuffer.put(coordinates);
    vertexBuffer.position(0);

    ByteBuffer ibb = ByteBuffer.allocateDirect(indexes.length *
    (Short.SIZE / 8));
    ibb.order(ByteOrder.nativeOrder());

    indexBuffer = ibb.asShortBuffer();
    indexBuffer.put(indexes);
    indexBuffer.position(0);

    ByteBuffer cbb = ByteBuffer.allocateDirect(colors.length *
    (Float.SIZE / 8));
    cbb.order(ByteOrder.nativeOrder());
```

```
colorBuffer = cbb.asFloatBuffer();
colorBuffer.put(colors);
colorBuffer.position(0);

Log.i(TAG, "Loaded obj with " + coordinates.length + " vertices &"
+ (indexes.length/3) + " faces");
}
```

Once we've set all the data to the 3DObject, we can prepare it to render by calling its `prepare()` method. This method will create the vertex and index Buffer, and, as in this case we don't have any color information from the mesh on the data file, it'll generate a random color, or rather an intensity, for each vertex.

Creating the buffers here in the 3DObject itself allows us to render any kind of object. The Scene container doesn't know what kind of object or what kind of geometry is inside. We could easily extend this class with another type of 3DObject, as long as it handles its own rendering.

Finally, we've added a `render()` method to the 3DObject:

```
public void render(int shaderProgram, String posAttributeName, String
colAttributeName) {
    int positionHandle = GLES20.glGetAttribLocation(shaderProgram,
    posAttributeName);
    GLES20.glVertexAttribPointer(positionHandle, 3,
            GLES20.GL_FLOAT, false,
            3 * 4, vertexBuffer);

    int colorHandle = GLES20.glGetAttribLocation(shaderProgram,
    colAttributeName);
    GLES20.glVertexAttribPointer(colorHandle, 4,
            GLES20.GL_FLOAT, false,
            4 * 4, colorBuffer);


    GLES20.glEnableVertexAttribArray(colorHandle);
    GLES20.glEnableVertexAttribArray(positionHandle);
    GLES20.glDrawElements(
            GLES20.GL_TRIANGLES, indexes.length,
            GLES20.GL_UNSIGNED_SHORT, indexBuffer);

    GLES20.glDisableVertexAttribArray(positionHandle);
    GLES20.glDisableVertexAttribArray(colorHandle);
}
```

This method is responsible for enabling and disabling the right arrays and rendering itself. We get the `shader` attributes from the method parameters. Ideally, each object could have its own `shader`, but we didn't want to add that much complexity in this example.

In our `GLDrawer` class, we've also added a helper method to calculate a perspective frustrum matrix. One of the most used calls in OpenGL was `gluPerspective`, and NeHe, the author of many awesome OpenGL tutorials, created a function to convert `gluPerspective` to a `glFrustrum` call:

```
// source:
http://nehe.gamedev.net/article/replacement_for_gluperspective/21002/

private static void perspectiveFrustrum(float[] matrix, float fov, float
aspect, float zNear, float zFar) {
    float fH = (float) (Math.tan( fov / 360.0 * Math.PI ) * zNear);
    float fW = fH * aspect;

    Matrix.frustumM(matrix, 0, -fW, fW, -fH, fH, zNear, zFar);
}
```

As we don't need it anymore, we've removed all vertex and face index information from `GLDrawer` and simplified the `onDrawFrame()` method to now delegate the rendering of all objects to the `Scene` class, and, by default, to each individual `3DObject`:

```
@Override
public void onDrawFrame(GL10 unused) {
    angle = ((float) SystemClock.elapsedRealtime() - startTime) *
    0.02f;
    GLES20.glClearColor(1.0f, 0.0f, 0.0f, 1.0f);
    GLES20.glClear(GLES20.GL_COLOR_BUFFER_BIT |
    GLES20.GL_DEPTH_BUFFER_BIT);

    if (scene != null) {
        Matrix.setLookAtM(mViewMatrix, 0,
                0, 0, -4,
                0f, 0f, 0f,
                0f, 1.0f, 0.0f);

        Matrix.multiplyMM(mMVPMatrix, 0, mProjectionMatrix, 0,
        mViewMatrix, 0);
        Matrix.rotateM(mMVPMatrix, 0, angle, 0.8f, 2.f, 1.f);

        GLES20.glUseProgram(shaderProgram);

        int mMVPMatrixHandle = GLES20.glGetUniformLocation(shaderProgram,
    "uMVPMatrix");
        GLES20.glUniformMatrix4fv(mMVPMatrixHandle, 1, false,
```

```
        mMVPMatrix, 0);

        scene.render(shaderProgram, "vPosition", "aColor");
    }
}
```

Putting it all together, if we run this example, we'll get the following screen:

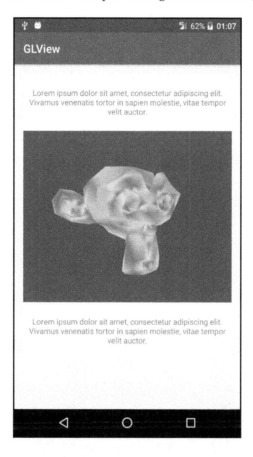

Check the `Example26-GLDrawing` on the GitHub repository for the full example source code.

Summary

In this chapter, we've seen how to create very basic custom views using OpenGL ES. OpenGL ES adds a lot of possibilities when creating custom views, but it also adds a lot of complexity if we don't have that much experience working with it. We could cover many more chapters on this topic, but that is not the main goal of this book. We'll have some more examples of using 3D custom views, but there is a lot of published material on how to learn, or even master, OpenGL ES on Android devices.

In the next chapter, we'll see how to add more animations and smooth movements to our custom view. As we could animate any parameter or variable, it will not matter if it is a 3D custom view or a standard 2D custom view, but we'll see how to apply animations in both cases.

6
Animations

So far we've seen how to create and render different types of custom views, from very simple 2D canvas drawing to more complex canvas operations, and recently how to create a custom view using OpenGL ES and vertex/fragment shaders. In some of the examples used to demonstrate how to use these rendering primitives, we've already used some animations and, as you could imagine, animations are one of the key elements of custom views. If we want to build a highly complex UI using a custom view, but we don't animate it at all, it might be better to simply use a static image.

In this chapter, we'll cover how to add animations to our custom views. There are many ways of doing it, but in more detail, we'll look at the following topics:

- Custom-made animations
- Fixed time step technique
- Using the Android Property Animator

In addition, we'll also see what are the issues if we implement some of the animations the wrong way, as it might seem simpler, and by just good luck, although it'll play against us, they'll seem to work perfectly fine on our device.

Custom-made animations

Let's start by showing how we can animate some values ourselves without relying too much on the methods and classes provided by the Android SDK. In this section, we'll see how to animate a single property or several properties using different mechanisms. By doing so, we could then apply the approach that suits us better on our custom views, depending on the type of animation we want to achieve or the specificities of the view we're implementing.

Timed frame animations

We have already used this kind of animation on the 3D example in our previous chapter. The main concept consists of assigning a new value to all the animatable properties before drawing a new frame based on the amount of time passed. We can be tempted with incrementing or computing a new value based on the number of frames drawn, but that is highly inadvisable, as the animation will be played at different speeds depending on the speed of the device, computation, or drawing complexity and other processes executing in the background.

To do it right, we have to involve something independent from the rendering speed, frames per second, or frames drawn, and a perfect solution is to use time-based animations.

Android provides us with several mechanisms to do so. For instance, we could use `System.currentTimeMillis()`, `System.nanoTime()`, or even some of the methods available in system clock, such as `elapsedRealtime()`.

Let's build a simple example comparing different methods. First, let's create a simple custom view that draws four rectangles, or `Rects`, rotated at different angles:

```
private static final int BACKGROUND_COLOR = 0xff205020;
private static final int FOREGROUND_COLOR = 0xffffffff;
private static final int QUAD_SIZE = 50;

private float[] angle;
private Paint paint;

public AnimationExampleView(Context context, AttributeSet attributeSet) {
    super(context, attributeSet);

    paint = new Paint();
    paint.setStyle(Paint.Style.FILL);
    paint.setAntiAlias(true);
    paint.setColor(FOREGROUND_COLOR);
    paint.setTextSize(48.f);

    angle = new float[4];
    for (int i = 0; i < 4; i++) {
        angle[i] = 0.f;
    }
}
```

On the class constructor, we initialize the `Paint` object and create an array of four floats to hold the angle of rotation of each rectangle. At this point, the four of them will be at 0. Let's now implement the `onDraw()` method.

On the `onDraw()` method, the first thing we've got to do is to clear the canvas background with a solid color, to clear our previous frame.

Once we've done so, we calculate the coordinates where we'll draw the four rectangles and proceed with the drawing. To simplify the rotation, in this case, we used the `canvas.translate` and `canvas.rotate` with a pivot point to rotate by the center of the rectangle. Also, to avoid doing additional calculations and keep it as simple as possible, we're surrounding each rectangle drawing with a `canvas.save` and `canvas.restore`, to keep the same state before each drawing operation:

```
@Override
protected void onDraw(Canvas canvas) {
    canvas.drawColor(BACKGROUND_COLOR);

    int width = getWidth();
    int height = getHeight();

    // draw 4 quads on the screen:
    int wh = width / 2;
    int hh = height / 2;

    int qs = (wh * QUAD_SIZE) / 100;

    // top left
    canvas.save();
    canvas.translate(
        wh / 2 - qs / 2,
        hh / 2 - qs / 2);

    canvas.rotate(angle[0], qs / 2.f, qs / 2.f);
    canvas.drawRect(0, 0, qs, qs, paint);
    canvas.restore();

    // top right
    canvas.save();
    canvas.translate(
        wh + wh / 2 - qs / 2,
        hh / 2 - qs / 2);

    canvas.rotate(angle[1], qs / 2.f, qs / 2.f);
    canvas.drawRect(0, 0, qs, qs, paint);
    canvas.restore();

    // bottom left
    canvas.save();
    canvas.translate(
        wh / 2 - qs / 2,
```

```
            hh + hh / 2 - qs / 2);

    canvas.rotate(angle[2], qs / 2.f, qs / 2.f);
    canvas.drawRect(0, 0, qs, qs, paint);
    canvas.restore();

    // bottom right
    canvas.save();
    canvas.translate(
        wh + wh / 2 - qs / 2,
        hh + hh / 2 - qs / 2);

    canvas.rotate(angle[3], qs / 2.f, qs / 2.f);
    canvas.drawRect(0, 0, qs, qs, paint);
    canvas.restore();

    canvas.drawText("a: " + angle[0], 16, hh - 16, paint);
    canvas.drawText("a: " + angle[1], wh + 16, hh - 16, paint);
    canvas.drawText("a: " + angle[2], 16, height - 16, paint);
    canvas.drawText("a: " + angle[3], wh + 16, height - 16, paint);

    postInvalidateDelayed(10);
}
```

To see the differences with more clarity, we're drawing a text showing the angle each rectangle is being rotated. And, to actually trigger a redraw of our view, we're calling an invalidate, delayed by 10 milliseconds.

The first rectangle will simply increment its angle each time it is drawn, ignoring time methods, and the other three will use respectively: System.currentTimeMillis(), System.nanoTime(), and SystemClock.elapsedRealtime(). Let's initialize some variables to hold the initial values of the timers:

```
private long timeStartMillis;
private long timeStartNanos;
private long timeStartElapsed;
```

Add a small calculation at the beginning of the onDraw() method:

```
if (timeStartMillis == -1)
    timeStartMillis = System.currentTimeMillis();

if (timeStartNanos == -1)
    timeStartNanos = System.nanoTime();

if (timeStartElapsed == -1)
    timeStartElapsed = SystemClock.elapsedRealtime();
```

```
angle[0] += 0.2f;
angle[1] = (System.currentTimeMillis() - timeStartMillis) * 0.02f;
angle[2] = (System.nanoTime() - timeStartNanos) * 0.02f * 0.000001f;
angle[3] = (SystemClock.elapsedRealtime() - timeStartElapsed) * 0.02f;
```

Since some time can pass from the initial class creation to when the onDraw() method is called, we're calculating the initial value of the timers here. If the value of timeStartElapsed is -1, for example, it means it has not been initialized.

Then, as we've set the initial time, we can compute how much time has passed and use that as the base value of our animations. Let's multiply it by a factor to control the speed. In this case, we've used 0.02 as an example, and took into account that nanoseconds are in another order of magnitude than milliseconds.

If we run this example, we'll have something similar to the following screenshot:

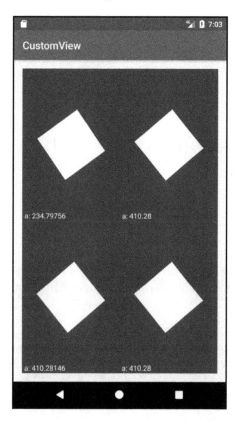

One of the issues with this approach is that if we put the application in the background and after some time we put it back on the foreground, we can see all the values depending on time jumping forward, as time will not stop when our app is in the background. To control this, we can override the `onVisibilityChanged()` callback and check whenever our view is visible or invisible:

```
@Override
protected void onVisibilityChanged(@NonNull View changedView, int
visibility) {
    super.onVisibilityChanged(changedView, visibility);

    // avoid doing this check before View is even visible
    if ((visibility == View.INVISIBLE || visibility == View.GONE) &&
        previousVisibility == View.VISIBLE) {

        invisibleTimeStart = SystemClock.elapsedRealtime();
    }

    if ((previousVisibility == View.INVISIBLE || previousVisibility ==
        View.GONE) &&
        visibility == View.VISIBLE) {

        timeStartElapsed += SystemClock.elapsedRealtime() -
        invisibleTimeStart;
    }
    previousVisibility = visibility;
}
```

In the preceding code, we're calculating the time our view is not visible and adjusting the `timeStartElapsed` with that time. We've to avoid doing it the very first time, as this method will be called the first time the view becomes visible. For that reason, we're checking if `timeStartElapsed` is different from −1.

As we have this callback just before our view becomes visible, we can easily change our previous code to calculate the initial value of the timers and put it here, simplifying our `onDraw()` method as well:

```
@Override
protected void onVisibilityChanged(@NonNull View changedView, int
visibility) {
    super.onVisibilityChanged(changedView, visibility);

    // avoid doing this check before View is even visible
    if (timeStartElapsed != -1) {
        if ((visibility == View.INVISIBLE || visibility == View.GONE)
            &&
```

```
            previousVisibility == View.VISIBLE) {

                invisibleTimeStart = SystemClock.elapsedRealtime();
        }

        if ((previousVisibility == View.INVISIBLE || previousVisibility
            == View.GONE) &&
            visibility == View.VISIBLE) {

                timeStartElapsed += SystemClock.elapsedRealtime() -
                invisibleTimeStart;
        }
    } else {
        timeStartMillis = System.currentTimeMillis();
        timeStartNanos = System.nanoTime();
        timeStartElapsed = SystemClock.elapsedRealtime();
    }
    previousVisibility = visibility;
}
```

With this small adjustment, only to the `timeStartElapsed`, we'll see the animation is preserved on the bottom right rectangle even when we put the application in the background.

You can find the whole example source code in the `Example27-Animations` folder in the GitHub repository.

Fixed timestep

There are times when calculations can be very complex when dealing with animations. One clear example can be in physics simulations and in games in general, but some other times, our calculations, even for a simple-ish custom view, can get a bit tricky when using time-based animation. Having a fixed timestep will allow us to abstract our animation logic from time variables, but still keep our animation tied to time.

The logic behind having a fixed timestep is to assume our animation logic will be always executed a fixed rate. For instance, we can assume it will be executed at *60 fps* regardless of which is the actual rendering frames per second. To show how it could be done, we'll create a new custom view that will spawn particles at the position we're pressing or dragging on the screen and applying some very basic and simple physics.

First, let's create the basic custom view like our previous example:

```
private static final int BACKGROUND_COLOR = 0xff404060;
private static final int FOREGROUND_COLOR = 0xffffffff;
private static final int N_PARTICLES = 800;

private Paint paint;
private Particle[] particles;
private long timeStart;
private long accTime;
private int previousVisibility;
private long invisibleTimeStart;


public FixedTimestepExample(Context context, AttributeSet attributeSet) {
    super(context, attributeSet);

    paint = new Paint();
    paint.setStyle(Paint.Style.FILL);
    paint.setAntiAlias(true);
    paint.setColor(FOREGROUND_COLOR);

    particles = new Particle[N_PARTICLES];
    for (int i = 0; i < N_PARTICLES; i++) {
        particles[i] = new Particle();
    }

    particleIndex = 0;
    timeStart = -1;
    accTime = 0;
    previousVisibility = View.GONE;
}
```

We're initializing the basic variables and we're also creating an array of `particles`. Also, as we've implemented the `onVisibilityChange` callback on our previous example, let's take advantage of it:

```
@Override
protected void onVisibilityChanged(@NonNull View changedView, int
visibility) {
    super.onVisibilityChanged(changedView, visibility);
    if (timeStartElapsed != -1) {
        // avoid doing this check before View is even visible
        if ((visibility == View.INVISIBLE || visibility == View.GONE)
            &&
            previousVisibility == View.VISIBLE) {

            invisibleTimeStart = SystemClock.elapsedRealtime();
```

```
        }

        if ((previousVisibility == View.INVISIBLE || previousVisibility
            == View.GONE) &&
            visibility == View.VISIBLE) {

            timeStart += SystemClock.elapsedRealtime() -
            invisibleTimeStart;
        }
    } else {
        timeStart = SystemClock.elapsedRealtime();
    }
    previousVisibility = visibility;
}
```

Let's now define the `Particle` class, let's keep it as simple as possible:

```
class Particle {
    float x;
    float y;
    float vx;
    float vy;
    float ttl;

    Particle() {
        ttl = 0.f;
    }
}
```

We've only defined the x, y coordinates, the x and y velocity as vx and vy respectively, and the time to live of the particle. When the time to live of the particle reaches 0, we'll not update or draw it anymore.

Now, let's implement the `onDraw()` method:

```
@Override
protected void onDraw(Canvas canvas) {
    animateParticles(getWidth(), getHeight());

    canvas.drawColor(BACKGROUND_COLOR);

    for(int i = 0; i < N_PARTICLES; i++) {
        float px = particles[i].x;
        float py = particles[i].y;
        float ttl = particles[i].ttl;

        if (ttl > 0) {
            canvas.drawRect(
```

```
                    px - PARTICLE_SIZE,
                    py - PARTICLE_SIZE,
                    px + PARTICLE_SIZE,
                    py + PARTICLE_SIZE, paint);
        }
    }
    postInvalidateDelayed(10);
}
```

We've delegated all the animation to the `animateParticles()` method and here we're just iterating through all the particles, checking if their time to live is positive and, in that case, drawing them.

Let's see now how we can implement the `animateParticles()` method with a fixed time step:

```
private static final int TIME_THRESHOLD = 16;
private void animateParticles(int width, int height) {
    long currentTime = SystemClock.elapsedRealtime();
    accTime += currentTime - timeStart;
    timeStart = currentTime;

    while(accTime > TIME_THRESHOLD) {
        for (int i = 0; i < N_PARTICLES; i++) {
            particles[i].logicTick(width, height);
        }

        accTime -= TIME_THRESHOLD;
    }
}
```

We calculate the time difference from the last time, or delta of time, and we accumulate it in the `accTime` variable. Then, as long as `accTime` is higher than the threshold we've defined, we execute one logic step. It might happen that more than one logic steps are executed between renders or, in some other cases, it might not get executed during two different frames.

Finally, we subtract the time threshold we defined to the `accTime` for each logic step we've executed and we set the new `timeStart` to the time we used for calculating the difference of time from the previous call to `animateParticles()`.

In this example, we've defined the time threshold to be 16, so every 16 milliseconds we'll execute one logic step, independently if we're rendering 10 or 60 frames per second.

The `logicTick()` method on the `Particle` class completely ignores the current value of the timer, as it assumes it'll be executed on a fixed time step:

```
void logicTick(int width, int height) {
    ttl--;

    if (ttl > 0) {
        vx = vx * 0.95f;
        vy = vy + 0.2f;

        x += vx;
        y += vy;

        if (y < 0) {
            y = 0;
            vy = -vy * 0.8f;
        }

        if (x < 0) {
            x = 0;
            vx = -vx * 0.8f;
        }

        if (x >= width) {
            x = width - 1;
            vx = -vx * 0.8f;
        }
    }
}
```

It's an extreme over-simplification of a particle physic simulation. It basically applies friction and adds vertical acceleration to the particles, calculates if they have to bounce from the screen limits, and calculates the new x and y positions.

We're just missing the code to spawn new particles when we've a pressed or dragged a `TouchEvent`:

```
@Override
public boolean onTouchEvent(MotionEvent event) {
    switch (event.getAction()) {
        case MotionEvent.ACTION_DOWN:
        case MotionEvent.ACTION_MOVE:
            spawnParticle(event.getX(), event.getY());
            return true;
    }
    return super.onTouchEvent(event);
}
```

Here, we're calling `spawnParticle()` as long as we've got a touch event that is a press or a move. The implementation of `spawnParticle()` is also very simple:

```
private static final int SPAWN_RATE = 8;
private int particleIndex;

private void spawnParticle(float x, float y) {
    for (int i = 0; i < SPAWN_RATE; i++) {
        particles[particleIndex].x = x;
        particles[particleIndex].y = y;
        particles[particleIndex].vx = (float) (Math.random() * 40.f) -
        20.f;
        particles[particleIndex].vy = (float) (Math.random() * 20.f) -
        10.f;
        particles[particleIndex].ttl = (float) (Math.random() * 100.f)
        + 150.f;
        particleIndex++;
        if (particleIndex == N_PARTICLES) particleIndex = 0;
    }
}
```

We are using the `particleIndex` variable as a circular index of the `particles` array. Whenever it arrives at the end of the array it'll start again at the very beginning. This method sets the x and y coordinates of the touch event and it randomizes the velocity and time to live of each spawned particle. We've created a `SPAWN_RATE` constant to spawn multiple particles on the same touch event and improve the visual effect.

If we run the application, we can see it in action, and it'll be very similar to the following screenshot, but in this case, it's very hard to capture the idea of the animation in a screenshot:

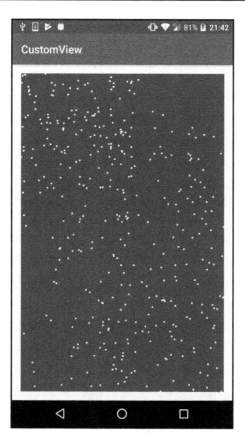

But we're missing something. As we've mentioned before, sometimes we'll execute two, or maybe more, logic steps between two rendered frames, but on some other times, we'll not execute any logic steps between two consecutive frames. If we don't execute any logic steps between those two frames, the result will be the same and a waste of CPU and battery life.

Even if we're between logic steps, that doesn't mean it hasn't passed any time between frames. Actually, we're somewhere between the previous calculated logic step and the next one. The good news is that we can actually calculate that, improving the smoothness of the animation and solving this issue at the same time.

Let's include this modification to the `animateParticles()` method:

```
private void animateParticles(int width, int height) {
    long currentTime = SystemClock.elapsedRealtime();
    accTime += currentTime - timeStart;
    timeStart = currentTime;
     while(accTime > TIME_THRESHOLD) {
```

```
            for (int i = 0; i < N_PARTICLES; i++) {
                particles[i].logicTick(width, height);
            }
             accTime -= TIME_THRESHOLD;
        }
         float factor = ((float) accTime) / TIME_THRESHOLD;
         for (int i = 0; i < N_PARTICLES; i++) {
             particles[i].adjustLogicStep(factor);
         }
    }
```

We're calculating the factor between which will tell us how close or far it is from the next logic step. If the factor is 0, it means we're just at the exact time of the logic step we've just executed. If the factor is 0.5, it means we're halfway between the current step and the next one and if the factor is 0.8, we're almost at the next logic step and precisely *80% of time* passed since the previous step. The way to smooth the transition between one logic step and the next is to interpolate using this factor, but to be able to do so, first we need to calculate the values of the next step as well. Let's change the logicTick() method to implement this change:

```
float nextX;
float nextY;
float nextVX;
float nextVY;

void logicTick(int width, int height) {
    ttl--;

    if (ttl > 0) {
        x = nextX;
        y = nextY;
        vx = nextVX;
        vy = nextVY;

        nextVX = nextVX * 0.95f;
        nextVY = nextVY + 0.2f;

        nextX += nextVX;
        nextY += nextVY;

        if (nextY < 0) {
            nextY = 0;
            nextVY = -nextVY * 0.8f;
        }

        if (nextX < 0) {
            nextX = 0;
```

```
              nextVX = -nextVX * 0.8f;
          }

          if (nextX >= width) {
              nextX = width - 1;
              nextVX = -nextVX * 0.8f;
          }
      }
  }
```

Now, at every logic step we're assigning the values of the next logic step to the current variables to avoid recalculating them, and calculating the next logic step. This way, we've got both values; the current and the new values after the next logic step is executed.

As we'll be using some intermediate values between x, y, and nextX, nextY, we'll calculate these values on new variables as well:

```
  float drawX;
  float drawY;

  void adjustLogicStep(float factor) {
      drawX = x * (1.f - factor) + nextX * factor;
      drawY = y * (1.f - factor) + nextY * factor;
  }
```

As we can see, drawX and drawY will be an intermediate state between the current logic step and the next one. If we apply the previous example values to this factor, we'll see how this method works.

If factor is 0 drawX and drawY are exactly x and y. On the contrary, if factor is 1, drawX and drawY are exactly nextX and nextY, although this should never happen as another logic step would have been triggered.

In the case of factor being 0.8, drawX and drawY values are a linear interpolation weighed at *80%* the values of the next logic step and *20%* of the current one, allowing a smooth transition between states.

You can find the whole example source code in the Example28-FixedTimestep folder in the GitHub repository. The fixed timestep is covered with more details in the fix your timestep artiche on the Gaffer On Games blog.

Using Android SDK Classes

So far, we've seen how to create our own animations, using time-based animations or using a fixed time step mechanism. But Android provides us several ways of doing animations using its SDK and the animation framework. In most cases, we can simplify our animations by just using the property animator system instead of creating our own, but that will depend, always, on the complexity of what we want to achieve and how we want to tackle the development.

For more information please refer to the property animation framework from the Android developer's documentation website.

ValueAnimator

As part of the property animator system, we have the `ValueAnimator` class. We can use it to simply animate `int`, `float`, or `color` variables or properties. It's quite easy to use, for instance we can animate a float value from `0` to `360` during `1500` milliseconds using the following code:

```
ValueAnimator angleAnimator = ValueAnimator.ofFloat(0, 360.f);
angleAnimator.setDuration(1500);
angleAnimator.start();
```

This is alright, but if we want to get updates of the animation and react to them, we've got to set an `AnimatorUpdateListener()`:

```
final ValueAnimator angleAnimator = ValueAnimator.ofFloat(0, 360.f);
angleAnimator.setDuration(1500);
angleAnimator.addUpdateListener(new ValueAnimator.AnimatorUpdateListener()
{
    @Override
    public void onAnimationUpdate(ValueAnimator animation) {
        angle = (float) angleAnimator.getAnimatedValue();
        invalidate();
    }
});
angleAnimator.start();
```

Also, in this example, we can see we're calling `invalidate()` from the `AnimatorUpdateListener()`, so we're also telling the UI to redraw the view.

There are many things we can configure of the way the animation behaves: from the animation repeat mode, number of repetitions, and type of interpolator. Let's see it in action using the same example we used at the beginning of this chapter. Let's draw four rectangles on the screen, and rotate them using different settings of a `ValueAnimator`:

```
//top left
final ValueAnimator angleAnimatorTL = ValueAnimator.ofFloat(0, 360.f);
angleAnimatorTL.setRepeatMode(ValueAnimator.REVERSE);
angleAnimatorTL.setRepeatCount(ValueAnimator.INFINITE);
angleAnimatorTL.setDuration(1500);
angleAnimatorTL.addUpdateListener(new
ValueAnimator.AnimatorUpdateListener() {
    @Override
    public void onAnimationUpdate(ValueAnimator animation) {
        angle[0] = (float) angleAnimatorTL.getAnimatedValue();
        invalidate();
    }
});

//top right
final ValueAnimator angleAnimatorTR = ValueAnimator.ofFloat(0, 360.f);
angleAnimatorTR.setInterpolator(new DecelerateInterpolator());
angleAnimatorTR.setRepeatMode(ValueAnimator.RESTART);
angleAnimatorTR.setRepeatCount(ValueAnimator.INFINITE);
angleAnimatorTR.setDuration(1500);
angleAnimatorTR.addUpdateListener(new
ValueAnimator.AnimatorUpdateListener() {
    @Override
    public void onAnimationUpdate(ValueAnimator animation) {
        angle[1] = (float) angleAnimatorTR.getAnimatedValue();
        invalidate();
    }
});

//bottom left
final ValueAnimator angleAnimatorBL = ValueAnimator.ofFloat(0, 360.f);
angleAnimatorBL.setInterpolator(new AccelerateDecelerateInterpolator());
angleAnimatorBL.setRepeatMode(ValueAnimator.RESTART);
angleAnimatorBL.setRepeatCount(ValueAnimator.INFINITE);
angleAnimatorBL.setDuration(1500);
angleAnimatorBL.addUpdateListener(new
ValueAnimator.AnimatorUpdateListener() {
    @Override
    public void onAnimationUpdate(ValueAnimator animation) {
        angle[2] = (float) angleAnimatorBL.getAnimatedValue();
        invalidate();
    }
```

```
    });

    //bottom right
    final ValueAnimator angleAnimatorBR = ValueAnimator.ofFloat(0, 360.f);
    angleAnimatorBR.setInterpolator(new OvershootInterpolator());
    angleAnimatorBR.setRepeatMode(ValueAnimator.REVERSE);
    angleAnimatorBR.setRepeatCount(ValueAnimator.INFINITE);
    angleAnimatorBR.setDuration(1500);
    angleAnimatorBR.addUpdateListener(new
    ValueAnimator.AnimatorUpdateListener() {
        @Override
        public void onAnimationUpdate(ValueAnimator animation) {
            angle[3] = (float) angleAnimatorBR.getAnimatedValue();
            invalidate();
        }
    });

    angleAnimatorTL.start();
    angleAnimatorTR.start();
    angleAnimatorBL.start();
    angleAnimatorBR.start();
```

Instead of setting the initial time and calculating the time difference, we're now configuring four different `ValueAnimators` and triggering the invalidate calls from their `onAnimationUpdate()` callbacks. On these `ValueAnimator`, we've used different interpolators and different repeat modes: `ValueAnimator.RESTART` and `ValueAnimator.REVERSE`. On all of them we've set the repeat count to `ValueAnimator.INFINITE` so we can observe and compare the details of the interpolator without pressure.

On the `onDraw()` method we've removed the `postInvalidate` call, as view will be invalidated by the animations, but leaving the `drawText()` it's very interesting, as we'll be able to see how the `OvershootInterpolator()` behaves and goes beyond their maximum value.

If we run this example, we'll see the four rectangles animating with different interpolation mechanisms. Play with the different interpolators, or even implement your own interpolator by extending TimeInterpolator and implement the `getInterpolation(float input)` method.

The input parameter of the `getInterpolation` method will be between 0 and 1, mapping 0 to the beginning of the animation and 1 to its end. The return value should be between 0 and 1, but could be lower or/and higher if we want to go beyond the original values like, for example, the `OvershootInterpolator`. The `ValueAnimator` will then compute the right value between the initial and final values based on this factor.

This example needs to be seen on an emulator or real device, but adding a bit of motion blur to the screenshot slightly shows the rectangles are animating at different speeds and accelerations.

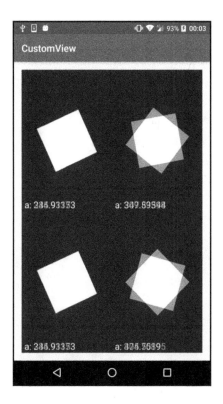

ObjectAnimator

If we want to animate objects directly instead of properties, we could use the `ObjectAnimator` class. `ObjectAnimator` is a subclass of `ValueAnimator` and uses the same functionality and features, but adds the ability to animate objects properties by name.

For instance, to show how it works, we could animate a property of our own View this way. Let's add a small rotation to the whole canvas, controlled by the `canvasAngle` variable:

```
float canvasAngle;

@Override
protected void onDraw(Canvas canvas) {
    canvas.save();
```

```
    canvas.rotate(canvasAngle, getWidth() / 2, getHeight() / 2);

    ...

    canvas.restore();
}
```

We've got to create a setter and a getter with the right name: `set<VariableName>`and `get<VariableName>` in camel case, and in our specific case:

```
public void setCanvasAngle(float canvasAngle) {
    this.canvasAngle = canvasAngle;
}

public float getCanvasAngle() {
    return canvasAngle;
}
```

As these methods will be called by the `ObjectAnimator`, as we've already created them, we're ready to set up the `ObjectAnimator` itself:

```
ObjectAnimator canvasAngleAnimator = ObjectAnimator.ofFloat(this,
"canvasAngle", -10.f, 10.f);
canvasAngleAnimator.setDuration(3000);
canvasAngleAnimator.setRepeatCount(ValueAnimator.INFINITE);
canvasAngleAnimator.setRepeatMode(ValueAnimator.REVERSE);
canvasAngleAnimator.addUpdateListener(new
ValueAnimator.AnimatorUpdateListener() {
    @Override
    public void onAnimationUpdate(ValueAnimator animation) {
        invalidate();
    }
});
```

It is basically the same approach of the `ValueAnimator`, but in this case, we're specifying the property to animate using a String and the reference to the object. As we've just mentioned, `ObjectAnimator` will call the getter and setter of the property using the `set<VariableName>` and `get<VariableName>` format. In addition, in the `onAnimationUpdate` callback there is only a call to `invalidate()`. We've removed any value assignation like on the previous examples, as it'll be automatically updated by the `ObjectAnimator`.

You can find the whole example source code in the `Example29-PropertyAnimation` folder in the GitHub repository.

Summary

In this chapter, we've seen how to add different types of animation to our custom views, from using the `ValueAnimator` and `ObjectAnimator` classes of the property animator system of Android, to creating our own animations using time-based animation or using a fixed time step mechanism.

Android provides us with even more animation classes, such as the `AnimatorSet` where we could combine several animations and specify which one plays before or after another.

As a recommendation, we shouldn't reinvent the wheel and, if it is enough, try to use what Android offers or maybe just extend it with our specific needs, but if it doesn't fit don't try to force it, as maybe building your own animation might be simple and easier to maintain.

As with everything when developing software, use common sense and choose the best option available.

In the next chapter, we'll see how to improve the performance of our custom views. In our custom views, we're in full control of the drawing, so optimizing the draw method and resource allocation is critical to avoid making our application sluggish and save some battery from the user.

7
Performance Considerations

In the previous chapters, we have been talking briefly about performance and, for example, avoiding doing some operations using the `onDraw()` method. But we haven't covered in detail why you should follow these recommendations and what the real impact of not following these best practices is to the custom view and to the application using it. Many of the things we will explain here might seem common sense, and indeed they should be, but sometimes we might not think about them, or we may not know or be aware of the real impact that it might have on the application, both from a performance point of view and regarding battery consumption.

In this chapter, we will address these points and we will look at the following topics in more detail:

- Recommendations and best practices
- The impact on the app when performance is not taken into account
- Code optimizations

Performance impact and recommendations

As we've just said, unless we have suffered it or we are supporting a low-end or really old device, we might not even be aware of what the impact is of not following the performance recommendations or best practices. If we are using a high-end device to test what are we currently developing, we might not see how it performs on a low-end device, and most probably there will be more downloads or more users using it on medium or low-end devices. It is almost the same as when we develop a network-connected piece of software with a nice and reliable Wi-Fi connection, or have an unlimited 4G network. The experience might not be the same for those with a limited or metered connection, and for especially those still on a 2G network.

It is important, in both cases, to take all our target users into account and test under several scenarios, with different devices and hardware.

The impact of not following the best practices

One of the recommendations we have been giving during these last chapters is to avoid allocating objects in the `onDraw()` method. But what will happen if we start allocating objects?

Let's create a simple custom view and allocate an object on purpose so we can evaluate the result when running the app:

```
package com.packt.rrafols.draw;

import android.content.Context;
import android.graphics.Bitmap;
import android.graphics.BitmapFactory;
import android.graphics.Canvas;
import android.graphics.Paint;
import android.graphics.Path;
import android.graphics.Rect;
import android.graphics.Region;
import android.util.AttributeSet;
import android.view.GestureDetector;
import android.view.MotionEvent;
import android.view.View;
import android.widget.Scroller;

public class PerformanceExample extends View {
    private static final String TAG =PerformanceExample.class.
                                    getName();

    private static final int BLACK_COLOR = 0xff000000;
    private static final int WHITE_COLOR = 0xffffffff;
    private float angle;

    public PerformanceExample(Context context, AttributeSet attributeSet)
    {
        super(context, attributeSet);

        angle = 0.f;
    }

    /**
     * This is precisely an example of what MUST be avoided.
     * It is just to exemplify chapter 7.
```

```
 *
 * DO NOT USE.
 *
 * @param canvas
 */
@Override
protected void onDraw(Canvas canvas) {
    Bitmap bitmap = Bitmap.createBitmap(getWidth(), getHeight(),
                    Bitmap.Config.ARGB_8888);
        Rect rect = new Rect(0, 0, getWidth(), getHeight());
        Paint paint = new Paint();
        paint.setColor(BLACK_COLOR);
        paint.setStyle(Paint.Style.FILL);
        canvas.drawRect(rect, paint);
        canvas.save();

        canvas.rotate(angle, getWidth() / 2, getHeight() / 2);
        canvas.translate((getWidth() - getWidth()/4) / 2,
                (getHeight() - getHeight()/4) / 2);

        rect = new Rect(0, 0, getWidth() / 4, getHeight() / 4);
        paint = new Paint();
        paint.setColor(WHITE_COLOR);
        paint.setStyle(Paint.Style.FILL);
        canvas.drawBitmap(bitmap, 0, 0, paint);
        canvas.drawRect(rect, paint);
        canvas.restore();
        invalidate();
        bitmap.recycle();
        angle += 0.1f;
    }
}
```

In this quick example, we are allocating several things within the onDraw() method, from the Paint objects, to the Rect objects, to creating a new bitmap, which allocates internal memory.

If we run this code, we'll get a rotating white rectangle in the middle of the screen, as in the following screenshot:

In addition, we will not only get a similar view. If we check the logcat logs when our application is running, we might get lines similar to these:

```
I art : Starting a blocking GC Explicit
I art : Explicit concurrent mark sweep GC freed 198893(13MB) AllocSpace
objects, 30(656KB) LOS objects, 26% free, 43MB/59MB, paused 2.835ms total
313.353ms
I art : Background partial concurrent mark sweep GC freed 26718(2MB)
AllocSpace objects, 1(20KB) LOS objects, 27% free, 43MB/59MB, paused
3.434ms total 291.430ms
```

We might even get them several times during the application execution. This is the Android run-time's (ART's) garbage collector kicking in to clean unused objects to free up some memory. As we are continuously creating new objects, the VM triggers the garbage collector to free up some memory.

More information about garbage collection can be found at the following URL: `https://en.wikipedia.org/wiki/Garbage_collection_(computer_science)`.

Luckily, Android Studio already shows us, quite clearly, that we are doing something wrong inside our `onDraw()` method:

```
29
30        /**
31         * This is precisely an example of what MUST be avoided.
32         * It is just to exemplify chapter 7.
33         *
34         * DO NOT USE.
35         *
36         * @param canvas
37         */
38        @Override
39 ●      protected void onDraw(Canvas canvas) {
40            Bitmap bitmap = Bitmap.createBitmap(getWidth(), getHeight(), Bitmap.Config.ARGB_8888);
```
Avoid object allocations during draw/layout operations (preallocate and reuse instead) less... (⌘F1)

You should avoid allocating objects during a drawing or layout operation. These are called frequently, so a smooth UI can be interrupted by garbage collection pauses caused by the object allocations.

The way this is generally handled is to allocate the needed objects up front and to reuse them for each drawing operation.

Some methods allocate memory on your behalf (such as `Bitmap.create`), and these should be handled in the same way.

```
51                                            (getHeight() - getHeight()/4) / 2);
52
53            rect = new Rect(0, 0, getWidth() / 4, getHeight() / 4);
54            paint = new Paint();
55            paint.setColor(WHITE_COLOR);
56            paint.setStyle(Paint.Style.FILL);
57            canvas.drawBitmap(bitmap, 0, 0, paint);
58            canvas.drawRect(rect, paint);
59
60            canvas.restore();
61            invalidate();
62
```

It also shows us what it might cause if we don't follow this recommendation. In this case, if the garbage collector kicks in, in the middle of a scroll or drawing, we might get some stuttering or, simply, a smooth animation might be seen as jumpy or not as smooth as it should be.

Check the full source code of this example, which shouldn't be followed, in the `Example30-Performance` folder in the GitHub repository. Please use it as an example of what should be avoided.

Code optimization

Allocating objects is not the only thing we should take into consideration when thinking about performance in our custom view. The amount of calculations, the type of calculations, the amount of primitives we are drawing, the amount of overdrawing, and the list of things we should check, is pretty big. In the end, most things are common sense: just don't recalculate values that we already have and maximize parts of the code that can be skipped if there are no changes required or, basically, try to reuse as much as possible what has been calculated on previous frames.

Let's compare two methods that convert YUV pixel data to RGB. It is not the most typical thing you'll have to do in a custom view, but it's perfect to show how performance can be impacted by reusing as much as we can and not recalculating what doesn't have to be recalculated.

When getting frames from the camera viewfinder in Android, they are usually in YUV format instead of RGB. More information about YUV can be found at the following URL: `https://en.wikipedia.org/wiki/YUV`.

We will start with a straightforward code and we will optimize it step by step to evaluate the impact of all the optimizations:

```
private static void yuv2rgb(int width, int height, byte[] yuvData,
    int[] rgbData) {
    int uvOffset = width * height;
    for (int i = 0; i < height; i++) {
        int u = 0;
        int v = 0;
        for (int j = 0; j < width; j++) {
            int y = yuvData[i * width + j];
            if (y < 0) y += 256;

            if (j % 2 == 0) {
                u = yuvData[uvOffset++];
                v = yuvData[uvOffset++];
            }

            if (u < 0) u += 256;
            if (v < 0) v += 256;

            int nY = y - 16;
            int nU = u - 128;
            int nV = v - 128;

            if (nY< 0) nY = 0;
```

```
            int nR = (int) (1.164 * nY + 2.018 * nU);
            int nG = (int) (1.164 * nY - 0.813 * nV - 0.391 * nU);
            int nB = (int) (1.164 * nY + 1.596 * nV);

            nR = min(255, max(0, nR));
            nG = min(255, max(0, nG));
            nB = min(255, max(0, nB));

            nR&= 0xff;
            nG&= 0xff;
            nB&= 0xff;

            int color = 0xff000000 | (nR<< 16) | (nG<< 8) | nB;
            rgbData[i * width + j] = color;
        }
    }
}
```

This version is based on the YUV-to-RGB converter, found at the following URL:
`https://searchcode.com/codesearch/view/2393/` and
`http://sourceforge.jp/projects/nyartoolkit-and/`.

We've used the floating point version here so that we can see, later on, the differences with
the fixed point version.

Now, let's create a small custom view that will transform, in every frame, a YUV image to
an RGB, set it into a `Bitmap`, and draw it on the screen:

```
@Override
protected void onDraw(Canvas canvas) {
    yuv2rgb(imageWidth, imageHeight, yuvData, rgbData);
    bitmap.setPixels(rgbData, 0, imageWidth, 0, 0, imageWidth,
    imageHeight);

    canvas.drawBitmap(bitmap, 0.f, 0.f, null);

    frames++;
    invalidate();
}
```

Let's also add a code to check the number of frames per second that our small code will
manage to draw. We will use this measurement to check the performance improvements on
the optimizations we'll be doing:

```
if (timeStart == -1) {
    timeStart = SystemClock.elapsedRealtime();
} else {
```

```
        long tdiff = SystemClock.elapsedRealtime() - timeStart;
        if (tdiff != 0) {
            float fps = ((float) frames * 1000.f) / tdiff;
            Log.d(TAG, "FPS: " + fps);
        }
    }
```

If we run this code as it is, on my device it measures 1.20 frames per second. The demo image used is a *1,000x1,500* image. Let's see what we can do to improve it.

To start, we can remove some unnecessary calculations:

```
    private static void yuv2rgb(int width, int height, byte[] yuvData,
        int[] rgbData) {
        int uvOffset = width * height;
        int offset = 0;
        for (int i = 0; i < height; i++) {
            int u = 0;
            int v = 0;
            for (int j = 0; j < width; j++) {
                int y = yuvData[offset];
                ...
                rgbData[offset] = color;

                offset++;
            }
        }
    }
```

Here, we've removed the two calculations of the pixel position and we are doing it by just a single increment at each pixel. In the previous case, it was doing the calculation `i * width + j` both for reading the `yuvData` and writing to `rgbData`. If we check the frames per second counter after this change, we'll notice it has slightly increased to 1.22. Not a huge improvement, but it's a start.

Now, we can see in the original implementation, the one used in the Android SDK, that the floating point operations are commented out in favor of fixed point operations. Floating point operations are usually costlier than plain integer operations. The performance of floating point operations has been improving quite a lot these last years with all the new hardware, but integer operations are still faster. We will not be able to get the same precision as with floating point operations, but we can get quite a good approximation by using fixed-point arithmetic.

More information about fixed-point arithmetic can be found at the following URL: https://en.wikipedia.org/wiki/Fixed-point_arithmetic.

When using fixed-point arithmetic, we have to define the number of bits of an integer value that will be used as the fixed point precision. The remaining bits will be used to actually store the integer value. Obviously, we'll have more precision as more bits we use to store it but, on the other hand, we'll have less bits to store the integer value. The idea is to multiply all constants and operations by a power of two number and, after doing all the operations, divide the result by the same number. As it's a power of two, we can easily perform a fast bitwise shift right operation instead of a costly divide.

For example, if we used a fixed point precision of 10 bits, we have to multiply all values by *1,024* or shift them 10 bits to the left and, at the end of all calculations, perform a right shift of 10 bits.

Let's apply this to these operations:

```
int nR = (int) (1.164 * nY + 2.018 * nU);
int nG = (int) (1.164 * nY - 0.813 * nV - 0.391 * nU);
int nB = (int) (1.164 * nY + 1.596 * nV);
```

We are transforming them into the following:

```
int nR = (int) (1192 * nY + 2066 * nU);
int nG = (int) (1192 * nY - 833 * nV - 400 * nU);
int nB = (int) (1192 * nY + 1634 * nV);
```

We can check that *1.164 * 1,024* is `1192` rounded up, and the same applies to all the other constants-we rounded the numbers to get the most valid approximation.

For the same reason, we have to change the following checks:

```
nR = min(255, max(0, nR));
nG = min(255, max(0, nG));
nB = min(255, max(0, nB));
```

We have to change the check with *255*255* multiplied by *1,024* of shifted `10` positions to the left:

```
nR = min(255 << 10, max(0, nR));
nG = min(255 << 10, max(0, nG));
nB = min(255 << 10, max(0, nB));
```

Add the division by *1,024* or right shift by `10` before using the values to output the color:

```
nR>>= 10;
nG>>= 10;
nB>>= 10;
```

Implementing these changes, even if we have added some more operations compared to the floating point version, improves our frames per second counter to *1.55*.

Another small optimization we can do is to avoid calculating the `luminance` factor of every component, as it's the same in each case. So let's replace this code:

```
int nR = (int) (1192 * nY + 2066 * nU);
int nG = (int) (1192 * nY - 833 * nV - 400 * nU);
int nB = (int) (1192 * nY + 1634 * nV);
```

With this one, which only calculates the `luminance` once:

```
int luminance = 1192 * nY;
int nR = (int)(luminance + 2066 * nU);
int nG = (int)(luminance - 833 * nV - 400 * nU);
int nB = (int)(luminance + 1634 * nV);
```

This should be optimized by most compilers; I'm not sure what the new compilers D8 and R8 will do, but with the current Java/Android tooling, it isn't optimized. By making this small change, we increase the frames per second counter to *1.59*.

The way this YUV file format works is that a pair of U and V chroma values are shared for two `luminance` values, so let's try to use this to our advantage to compute two pixels at the same time, avoiding additional checks and code overhead:

```
for(int j = 0; j < width; j += 2) {
    int y0 = yuvData[offset];
    if (y0 < 0) y0 += 256;

    int y1 = yuvData[offset + 1];
    if (y1 < 0) y1 += 256;

    u = yuvData[uvOffset++];
    v = yuvData[uvOffset++];
    if (u < 0) u += 256;
    if (v < 0) v += 256;

    int nY0 = y0 - 16;
    int nY1 = y1 - 16;
    int nU = u - 128;
    int nV = v - 128;

    if (nY0 < 0) nY0 = 0;
    if (nY1 < 0) nY1 = 0;

    int chromaR = 2066 * nU;
    int chromaG = -833 * nV - 400 * nU;
```

```
    int chromaB = 1634 * nV;

    int luminance = 1192 * nY0;
    int nR = (int) (luminance + chromaR);
    int nG = (int) (luminance + chromaG);
    int nB = (int) (luminance + chromaB);

    nR = min(255 << 10, max(0, nR));
    nG = min(255 << 10, max(0, nG));
    nB = min(255 << 10, max(0, nB));

    nR>>= 10;
    nG>>= 10;
    nB>>= 10;

    nR&= 0xff;
    nG&= 0xff;
    nB&= 0xff;

    rgbData[offset] = 0xff000000 | (nR<< 16) | (nG<< 8) | nB;

    luminance = 1192 * nY1;
    nR = (int) (luminance + chromaR);
    nG = (int) (luminance + chromaG);
    nB = (int) (luminance + chromaB);

    nR = min(255 << 10, max(0, nR));
    nG = min(255 << 10, max(0, nG));
    nB = min(255 << 10, max(0, nB));

    nR>>= 10;
    nG>>= 10;
    nB>>= 10;

    nR&= 0xff;
    nG&= 0xff;
    nB&= 0xff;

    rgbData[offset + 1] = 0xff000000 | (nR<< 16) | (nG<< 8) | nB;

    offset += 2;
}
```

We are now just calculating the chroma components once, and we've removed the check to get new U and V components only every two pixels. Doing these changes increased our frames per second counter to *1.77*.

As Java bytes range from -128 to 127, we've added some checks for negative numbers, but instead of doing these checks, we can do a quick bitwise AND operation (&):

```
for (int i = 0; i < height; i++) {
    for (int j = 0; j < width; j += 2) {
        int y0 = yuvData[offset    ] & 0xff;
        int y1 = yuvData[offset + 1] & 0xff;

        int u = yuvData[uvOffset++] & 0xff;
        int v = yuvData[uvOffset++] & 0xff;

        . . .

    }
}
```

That small change slightly increased our frames per second counter to *1.83*. But we can still optimize it a bit more. We have used 10 bits of fixed-point arithmetic precision, but, in this particular case, we might have enough using 8 bits of precision. Changing from 10 bits of precision to only 8 will save us one operation:

```
for (int i = 0; i < height; i++) {
  for (int j = 0; j < width; j += 2) {
        . . .
    int chromaR = 517 * nU;
    int chromaG = -208 * nV - 100 * nU;
    int chromaB = 409 * nV;

    int lum = 298 * nY0;

    nR = min(65280, max(0, nR));
    nG = min(65280, max(0, nG));
    nB = min(65280, max(0, nB));

    nR<<= 8;
    nB>>= 8;

    nR&= 0x00ff0000;
    nG&= 0x0000ff00;
    nB&= 0x000000ff;

    rgbData[offset] = 0xff000000 | nR | nG | nB;

        . . .

    offset += 2;
    }
}
```

We've updated all the constants to be multiplied by 256 instead of *1,024*, and we've updated the checks. The constant 65280 that appears on the code is 255 multiplied by 256. On the part of the code that we are shifting the values to in order to get the actual color components, we have to shift right the red component by 8 and shift it left by 16 to adjust it to the ARGB position in the color component, so we can just do one single shift operation of 8 bits left. It's even better on the green coordinate-we have to shift it right by 8 and shift it left by 8, so we can leave it as it is and not shift it at all. We still have to shift right the blue component by 8 positions.

We also had to update the masks to check that every component stays between its 0-255 range, but now the masks are shifted by the right bit position s0x00ff0000, 0x0000ff00, and 0x000000ff.

This change marginally improved our frames per second counter to *1.85*, but we can still go further. Let's try to get rid of all the shifts, checks, and masks. We could do that by using some pre-calculated tables that we'll calculate once at the creation of our custom view. Let's create this function to pre-calculate everything we need:

```
private static int[] luminance;
private static int[] chromaR;
private static int[] chromaGU;
private static int[] chromaGV;
private static int[] chromaB;

private static int[] clipValuesR;
private static int[] clipValuesG;
private static int[] clipValuesB;

private static void precalcTables() {
    luminance = new int[256];
    for (int i = 0; i <luminance.length; i++) {
        luminance[i] = ((298 * (i - 16)) >> 8) + 300;
    }
    chromaR = new int[256];
    chromaGU = new int[256];
    chromaGV = new int[256];
    chromaB = new int[256];
    for (int i = 0; i < 256; i++) {
        chromaR[i] = (517 * (i - 128)) >> 8;
        chromaGU[i] = (-100 * (i - 128)) >> 8;
        chromaGV[i] = (-208 * (i - 128)) >> 8;
        chromaB[i] = (409 * (i - 128)) >> 8;
    }

    clipValuesR = new int[1024];
    clipValuesG = new int[1024];
```

```
        clipValuesB = new int[1024];
        for (int i = 0; i < 1024; i++) {
            clipValuesR[i] = 0xFF000000 | (min(max(i - 300, 0), 255) << 16);
            clipValuesG[i] = min(max(i - 300, 0), 255) << 8;
            clipValuesB[i] = min(max(i - 300, 0), 255);
        }
    }
```

We are calculating the values for `luminance`, all chroma components, and finally the clipped, shifted, and masked values for everything. As `luminance` and some chromas might be negative, we've added a +300 value to the `luminance` value, as it'll be added to all values, and then adapted the `clipValues` tables to take that 300 offset into account. Otherwise, we might try to index an array with a negative index, and that would make our application crash. Checking whether the index is negative before accessing the array will kill all the performance optimizations, as we are trying to get rid, as much as possible, of all operations and checks.

Using these tables, our YUV-to-RGB converter code is reduced to the following:

```
        private static void yuv2rgb(int width, int height, byte[] yuvData,
            int[] rgbData) {
            int uvOffset = width * height;
            int offset = 0;

            for (int i = 0; i < height; i++) {
                for (int j = 0; j < width; j += 2) {
                int y0 = yuvData[offset ] & 0xff;
                int y1 = yuvData[offset + 1] & 0xff;

                int u = yuvData[uvOffset++] & 0xff;
                int v = yuvData[uvOffset++] & 0xff;

                int chR = chromaR[u];
                int chG = chromaGV[v] + chromaGU[u];
                int chB = chromaB[v];

                int lum = luminance[y0];
                int nR = clipValuesR[lum + chR];
                int nG = clipValuesG[lum + chG];
                int nB = clipValuesB[lum + chB];

                rgbData[offset] = nR | nG | nB;

                lum = luminance[y1];
                nR = clipValuesR[lum + chR];
                nG = clipValuesG[lum + chG];
                nB = clipValuesB[lum + chB];
```

```
        rgbData[offset + 1] = nR | nG | nB;

        offset += 2;
      }
    }
  }
```

With these changes, we get a *2.04* frames per second counter, or a *70%* increase of performance, compared with the original method. Anyway, this is only an example of how code can be optimized; if you really want to convert, in real-time, a YUV image to RGB, I suggest that you either check out a native C or C++ implementation or go for a GPU or render script approach.

Finally, if we run this application, we will get a screen similar to the following screenshot. We are not scaling or applying any additional transformation to the image, as we just wanted to measure the amount of time that it takes to transform from a YUV image to an RGB image. Your screen image might differ depending on the screen size and your device:

Check the whole example source code in the `Example31-Performance` folder in the GitHub repository.

There are many other things to take into consideration when talking about performance. If you want to know more details about how Java code is translated into dexbyte code and executed in the Android VM, check out the following presentation: `https://www.slideshare.net/RaimonRls/the-bytecode-mumbojumbo`.

Mocking up the preview window

When previewing our custom views on Android Studio, there are some occasions when calculations can be very complex or, for example, we need some data initialized, but we can't do that while showing our custom view inside the preview window of Android Studio. We'll be able to do something about this by checking the `isInEditMode()` method.

This method will return true if we are inside an IDE or a development tool. Knowing this information, we could easily mock some of the data or simplify the rendering to just show a preview of what we want to draw.

For example, in the `Example07-BuilderPattern` folder in the GitHub repository, we are calling this method at the custom view creation to alter the color values used in the gradient, although we could actually call it during the `onDraw()` method as well, to alter the rendering of the view:

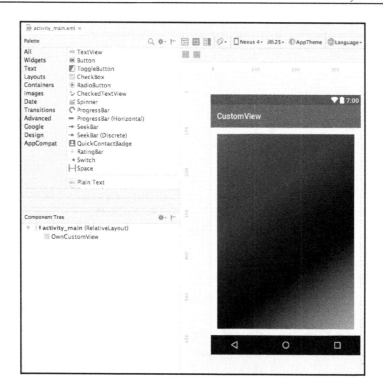

Summary

In this chapter, we have seen what the impact is of not following the performance recommendations and why there is a set of best practices and things we should avoid when implementing our own custom view. We have also seen how to improve or optimize a code for performance and how to tweak or customize a view to render a preview on the Android Studio IDE preview window.

As we will see in the next chapter, whether our custom view is used by other people or even by ourselves shouldn't make a difference. It should not make the application using it crash or misbehave because of it. Like including a third-party library, it should never crash our application, as otherwise, we will most probably stop using it and replace it with another library.

So, in the next chapter, we will not only see how to apply these recommendations, but also how to make our custom view reusable with many applications, and how to share it or open source it so it can be widely used within the Android community.

8
Sharing Our Custom View

We've been building our custom view, or many of them, in these last chapters. We've seen how to interact with them, how to draw 2D and 3D primitives, and we want somebody else to be able to use it. That is a great idea! It might be for ourselves, we might reuse it in a future project, or it might be a project by one of our colleagues. If we aim higher, it might be a project by the Android community.

One of the things that makes the Android community awesome is that there are lots of open source libraries. All these contributions by developers have helped many other developers get started in Android development, learn to get a deeper understanding of some concepts, or be able to build their applications in the first place.

Firstly, publishing your custom view or, for instance, an Android library, is one of the methods that contributes to this amazing community. Secondly, by doing so, it's a great way to advertise yourself, show the openness of your employer, and also attract talent to your company.

In this chapter, we'll see what we should take into consideration if we want to share our custom view and how to do it. We'll also put into practice some of the important recommendations we've given in the previous chapters. Even more importantly, we want other developers to use our custom view.

In more detail, we'll cover the following topics:

- Recommendations and best practices
- Publishing your custom view

Almost all recommendations given can be applied not only to custom views but to any Android library we'd like to share or we want to make reusable for our colleagues or other projects.

Best practices for sharing our custom view

We should always aim for the highest quality possible, even though we're building a custom view or component only for ourselves or for a small application. However, there are some additional checks and best practices that we've to take into account if we want to share our custom view so others can use it. If that is our goal, and we'd like to get as many developers as possible using it in their applications or contributing to it, it'll be quite challenging to involve them if we ignore these basic recommendations.

Considerations and recommendations

Something we should consider is that once we share our custom view, it might be used for many Android applications. If our custom view has errors and crashes, it'll crash the application using it. The application's users will not consider the custom view at fault but rather the application itself. The application developer, or developers, might try to open an issue or even submit a pull request to fix it, but if the custom view gives them too much trouble, they'll just replace it.

This applies to your own applications as well; you don't want to use an unstable component or custom view as you might end up either rewriting it or patching it up. As we've just mentioned, we should always aim for the highest quality. If our custom view is only used in one single application, the impact of finding a critical issue once it's at the production stage or the application is published to the store or stores only affects one application. However, if it's used by several applications, the impact and cost of maintenance increases. You can imagine the impact of detecting a highly critical issue of an open source component and having to make new releases of all the applications using it.

In addition, you should try to keep your code clean, well-organized, properly tested, and reasonably documented. It'll be easier for you, as well as your colleagues if you're sharing the custom view at your company, to maintain the custom view, and if it's open source, it will encourage contributions and won't actually scare external contributors. As with many other things, common sense applies. Don't over-document your custom view as basically nobody will read it; keep it as simple as possible and straight to the point.

In the following screenshot, we can see the open issues of the `retrofit` library, an open source Android library widely used in many applications:

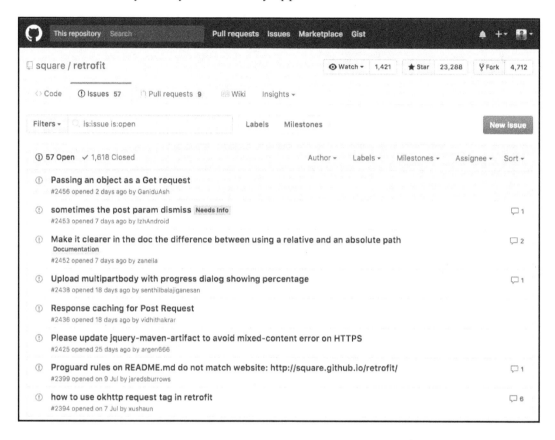

Also, we can see there are many pull requests submitted by several developers, either fixing issues or adding functionality or features. In the following screenshot is an example of a pull request submitted to the `retrofit` library:

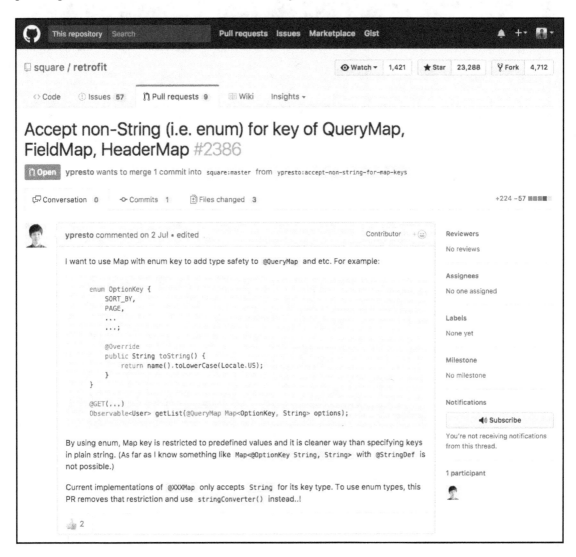

We've previously covered it already, but it's also important that the custom view behaves properly. Not only must it be crash-free but it also has to work properly on several devices and resolutions and have good performance.

We can sum up the list of recommendations with the following points:

- Stable
- Work across devices and resolutions
- Performant
- Developed applying best code practices and standard style
- Properly documented and easy to use

Configurable

We've explained in `Chapter 2`, *Implementing Your First Custom View*, how to parameterize a custom view. We've created it because it might serve a very specific purpose, but in general the more configurable it is, the more likely it will be used somewhere else.

Imagine we're building a progress bar. If our custom view always draws a horizontal red bar, it'll have its uses but not many as it's too specific. If we allow the developer of the application using this custom view to customize the color of the bar, we'd add several other use cases for it. If, in addition, we also allow developers to configure the background color or what kind of primitive we're drawing instead of a horizontal bar, we'll cover even more different scenarios with our custom view.

We need to be careful as well; adding so many options will also increase the complexity of the code and the component itself. Configuring colors is straightforward and doesn't have that much impact, but being able to change the drawing primitive, for example, might be slightly trickier. Adding complexity might impact on performance, stability, and our ability to test and verify all scenarios are working fine when publishing it or making a new release.

Publishing our custom view

Once we're happy with our custom view and the way it is, we're ready to share it. If we've also followed the best practices and recommendations, we might be additionally confident. Even if you haven't, the best way to learn is to get feedback from the community as soon as possible. Don't be afraid of making mistakes; you'll learn on the way.

There are many ways of publishing a custom view: we can open source it, for example, or we can just publish a compiled binary as a SDK or Android library. Most of the recommendations above are given for the open source approach or internal reuse, either for yourself or your colleagues, but many of them, not all, also apply if your goal is to publish a closed SDK or just the compiled binary as a library.

Open sourcing our custom view

Open sourcing a custom view or, alternatively, an Android library, is pretty easy and straightforward. You need to make sure you perform some additional steps but the process itself is very simple.

We've been using GitHub to share the source code of the examples of this book. This is not a coincidence. GitHub is one of the most widely used tools for sharing source code and open source libraries and projects. It's also the tool we will recommend and will use in this chapter to explain how to publish our custom view.

First things first; if we don't have a GitHub account, we've to register ourselves and create it. Creating an account is free as long as we want to host only public repositories or publicly accessible code. If we want to use it to store private code repositories, we've the paid option. For the scope of this book, we've more than enough with the free option.

We can register directly from the home page: `https://www.github.com` or from: `https://github.com/join`.

Once we have made the account, we create a code repository to store the code. We can do so at:
`https://github.com/new`.
As shown in following screenshot:

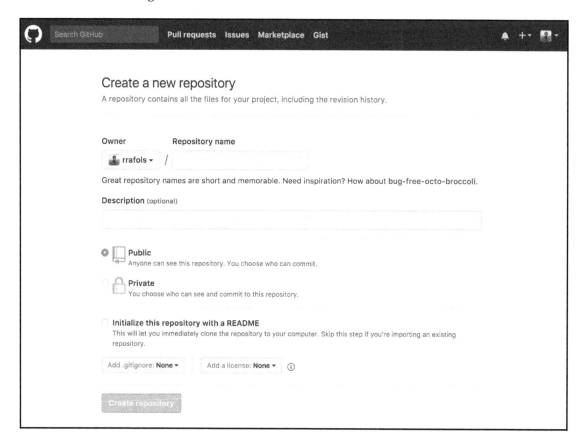

We must choose a repository name. It is highly recommended to add a description so its easier for everyone else to understand what our component or library is doing. We also have the option of adding a `.gitignore` file and adding a license.

The `.gitignore` is quite a useful file. All files mentioned here won't be uploaded to GitHub. For instance, there is no need to upload all the temporary files, builds, intermediate build files, or configuration files from Android Studio that hold information about the project specifically to our local computer. It won't be useful to anybody to know that we're storing the project in `\Users\raimon\development\AndroidCustomView` for instance.

Adding a license is very important to determine what rights we are granting to those using our source code. Some of the most common licenses for open source projects are Apache 2.0, MIT, and GPLv3 licenses:

- MIT is the less restrictive and permissive license. It allows other parties to use the source in any way they want as long as they include the license and copyright notice.
- Apache 2.0 is also quite permissive. Like the MIT license, it allows other parties to use the source in any way they want as long as they include the license and copyright notice and state the changes done to the original files.
- GPLv3 is slightly more restrictive as it forces anyone using your source code to distribute the source code of the application using it under the same license. This might be a restriction for some companies as they'd like to preserve the IP of their source code.

All three licenses limit the liability of the original developer and do not provide any warranty. They all provide the software or source code as is.

Many Android libraries use either the MIT or Apache 2.0 license and it's our recommendation to use either for your custom view.

Once the repository is created and initialized, we can upload our code. We can use any Git client we prefer or simply use the command-line interface.

First, we clone the repository we've just created-just as reference, not a real repository:

```
raimon$ git clone https://github.com/rrafols/androidcustomview.git
Cloning into 'androidcustomview'...
remote: Counting objects: 5, done.
remote: Compressing objects: 100% (4/4), done.
remote: Total 5 (delta 0), reused 0 (delta 0), pack-reused 0
Unpacking objects: 100% (5/5), done.
```

Checking connectivity. Done.

If we already have the directory created with our source code inside, Git will complain it can't create the directory:

```
raimon$ git clone https://github.com/rrafols/androidcustomview.git
```

fatal: destination path `androidcustomview` already exists and is not an empty directory.

In this case, we've to use a different approach. First, we have to initialize the local repository:

```
androidcustomview raimon$ gitinit
Initialized empty Git repository in
/Users/raimon/dev/androidcustomview/.git/
```

Then add the remote repository:

```
androidcustomview raimon$ git remote add origin
https://github.com/rrafols/androidcustomview.git
```

Finally, pull the content from the master branch:

```
androidcustomview raimon$ git pull origin master
remote: Counting objects: 5, done.
remote: Compressing objects: 100% (4/4), done.
remote: Total 5 (delta 0), reused 0 (delta 0), pack-reused 0
Unpacking objects: 100% (5/5), done.
From https://github.com/rrafols/androidcustomview
 * branch              master       -> FETCH_HEAD
 * [new branch]        master       -> origin/master
```

Now we can add all the files we'd like to add to the GitHub repository. In this case, we'll add everything and Git will automatically ignore those files matching the patterns on the .gitignore file:

```
androidcustomview raimon$ git add *
```

We can commit to the local repository now. Always use a meaningful commit message or description as it will be useful later on to know what was changed:

```
androidcustomview raimon$ git commit -m "Adding initial files"
[master bc690c7] Adding initial files
 6 files changed, 741 insertions(+)
```

When this is done, we're ready to push those commits to the remote repository, at https:// github.com/ in this example:

```
androidcustomview raimon$ git push origin master
Username for 'https://github.com': rrafols
Password for 'https://rrafols@github.com':
Counting objects: 9, done.
Delta compression using up to 4 threads.
Compressing objects: 100% (8/8), done.
Writing objects: 100% (8/8), 6.06 KiB | 0 bytes/s, done.
Total 8 (delta 3), reused 0 (delta 0)
remote: Resolving deltas: 100% (3/3), done.
```

```
To https://github.com/rrafols/androidcustomview.git
343509f..bc690c7 master -> master
```

For more information about Git go to:
`https://en.wikipedia.org/wiki/Git`.

When creating a repository, GitHub also asks us if we wants to create a README.md file. This README.md file is what will be shown on the repository page as documentation. It's formatted using markdown, which is why the extension is .md, and it's important to keep it up-to-date with information about the project, how to use it, a quick example, and a mention of the license and authors. The most important part here is that anyone who wants to use your custom view can check quite quickly how to do so, if the license is appropriate, and how to contact you for support and help. This last part is optional as they can always open an issue on GitHub, but it's nice to have. We can even edit and preview the changes directly from:
`https://github.com/`.

It's not only important to keep the documentation up-to-date, it's also important to keep the library maintained and up-to-date. There are bugs that need addressing, new features to add, new versions of Android that break, deprecate, improve or add new method, and other developers opening issues or asking questions. When looking for a custom view or Android library, if there are no recent updates or, at least, not in the last few months, it looks abandoned and it greatly decreases the chances somebody else will use it.

Creating a binary artifact

We've been talking about shared custom views and Android libraries as if they were the same. The most suitable way to share a custom view is as an Android library. The main difference between an Android application and an Android library is that the latter cannot be run by itself on a device or emulator and will only produce an .aar file. This .aar file can, later on, be added as a dependency in an Android application project or other libraries. We could also have sub-modules inside the same project and have dependencies between them. To see how this works, we'll convert a custom view project into an Android library and we'll add a test application project to quickly test it.

First, once we have an Android application, we can convert it to a library by just performing two simple steps:

1. Remove the line mentioning the `applicationId` on the app module `build.gradle` file.

2. Change the plugin applied from `com.android.application` to `com.android.library`.

Basically changing the following:

```
apply plugin: 'com.android.application'

android {
    compileSdkVersion 25
    buildToolsVersion"25.0.2"
    defaultConfig {
        applicationId"com.rrafols.packt.customview"
        minSdkVersion 21
        targetSdkVersion 25
        versionCode 1
        versionName"1.0"
```

Change to the following:

```
apply plugin: 'com.android.library'

android {
    compileSdkVersion 25
    buildToolsVersion"25.0.2"
     defaultConfig {
        minSdkVersion 21
        targetSdkVersion 25
        versionCode 1
        versionName"1.0"
```

In our example, we've also refactored the app module name to lib.

More information on how to convert an Android application to an Android library can be found at the developer Android documentation page:

`https://developer.android.com/studio/projects/android-library.html.`

If we're developing or extending this library, we'd recommend adding a new module inside the project as a test application. It would considerably speed up developing and testing of the custom view.

We can add a new module using the Android Studio File menu: **File** | **New** | **New Module**:

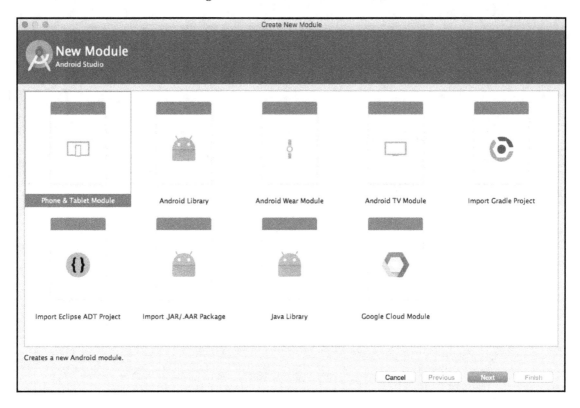

Once we've added a test application module, we add a dependency to the library. In the `build.gradle` file of the new module, add a dependency to the local lib module:

```
dependencies {
    compile project(":lib")
    compile fileTree(dir: 'libs', include: ['*.jar'])
    androidTestCompile('com.android.support.test.espresso:espresso-
core:2.2.2',
    {
        exclude group: 'com.android.support', module: 'support-annotations'
    })

    compile 'com.android.support:appcompat-v7:25.3.1'
    compile 'com.android.support.constraint:constraint-layout:1.0.2'
    testCompile'junit:junit:4.12'
}
```

Now you can add the custom view to this new test application layout and test it. In addition, we can also produce a library binary to distribute. It'll only include the library or the lib module. We can do so by executing the `lib:assembleRelease` task on gradle:

```
Example32-Library raimon$ ./gradlew lib:assembleRelease
```

We'll get the `.aar` file in our project folder at `lib/build/outputs/aar/lib-release.aar`. Using the `lib:assembleDebug` task, we'll produce the debug library, or simply using `lib:assembleDebug` we'll get both debug and release versions.

You can distribute the binary in any way you prefer, but one recommendation is to upload to an artifact platform. Many companies are using internal artifact or software repositories for their enterprise libraries and artifacts in general, but if you want to make it available to the wider public, you can upload it to `JCenter`, for example. If we check our topmost `build.gradle` file from any Android project, we will see there is a dependency on `JCenter` to look for libraries:

```
...
repositories {
    jcenter()
}
```

We can easily do so from Bintray: `https://bintray.com`, for example. Once we've registered, we could create projects, import them from GitHub, create releases and versions, and even publish it to `JCenter` if our project is accepted.

For more information about the Bintray gradle plugin, go to:
`https://github.com/bintray/gradle-bintray-plugin#readme`.

To simplify our lives, there are some open source examples and code that will make this process way simpler. But first, let's create a repository on Bintray.

We'll name it `AndroidCustomView`, set it up as a Maven repository, and add a default Apache 2.0 license:

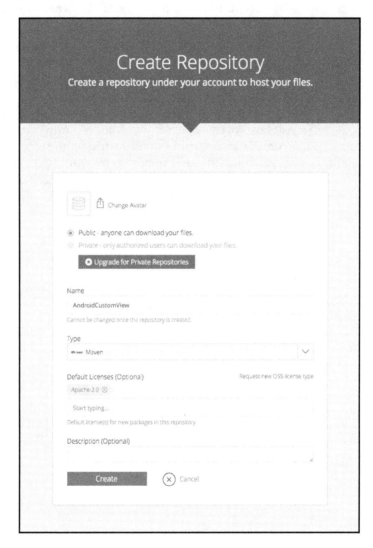

Once we have it, we can create versions or we can add them directly from our gradle build scripts. In order to do so, we must add some dependencies to our topmost `build.gradle`:

```
buildscript {
    repositories {
        jcenter()
    }

    dependencies {
        classpath'com.android.tools.build:gradle:2.3.0'
        classpath'com.jfrog.bintray.gradle:gradle-
bintrayplugin:1.4'classpath'com.github.dcendents:android-maven-
gradleplugin:1.4.1'
    }
}
```

Now we can take advantage of some open source gradle build scripts already created. Instead of copying and pasting or adding more code to our build script, we can simply apply it directly from GitHub. Let's add these two lines to the very end of our library `build.gradle` file:

```
...
apply from:
'https://raw.githubusercontent.com/nuuneoi/JCenter/master/installv1.gra
  dle'
apply from:
'https://raw.githubusercontent.com/nuuneoi/JCenter/master/bintrayv1.gra
  dle'
```

After applying these two gradle build scripts, we end up having an additional task: `bintrayUpload`. We need to add the artifact configuration first, so let's add it at the very beginning of the file, just after the apply library line on the library module `build.gradle` file:

```
apply plugin: 'com.android.library'

ext {
    bintrayRepo = 'AndroidCustomView'
    bintrayName = 'androidcustomview'
    publishedGroupId = 'com.rrafols.packt'
    libraryName = 'AndroidCustomView'
    artifact = 'androidcustomview'
    libraryDescription = 'Uploading libraries example.'
    siteUrl = 'https://github.com/rrafols/AndroidCustomView'
    gitUrl = 'https://github.com/rrafols/androidcustomview.git'
    libraryVersion = '1.0.0'
    developerId = 'rrafols'
```

```
        developerName = 'Raimon Ràfols'
        developerEmail = ''
        licenseName = 'The Apache Software License, Version 2.0'
        licenseUrl = 'http://www.apache.org/licenses/LICENSE-2.0.txt'
        allLicenses = ["Apache-2.0"]
    }
```

We need to add the Bintray user and API key information to our `local.properties` file:

```
bintray.user=rrafols
bintray.apikey=<key - can be retrieved from the edit profile option on
bintray.com>
```

The `bintrayRepo` variable has to match the repository where we'd like to store our binaries or otherwise the build script will fail.

Now that we've all the configuration in place, we can build a new version of the library by using `./gradlew` install and uploading it to Bintray by using `./gradlew bintrayUpload`.

Keep in mind that versions are read-only when they've been uploaded, so we'll not be able to override them and we'll get an error when executing our gradle script unless we update the version number and upload a different version.

Once we've uploaded a version, we'll have something close to the following screen:

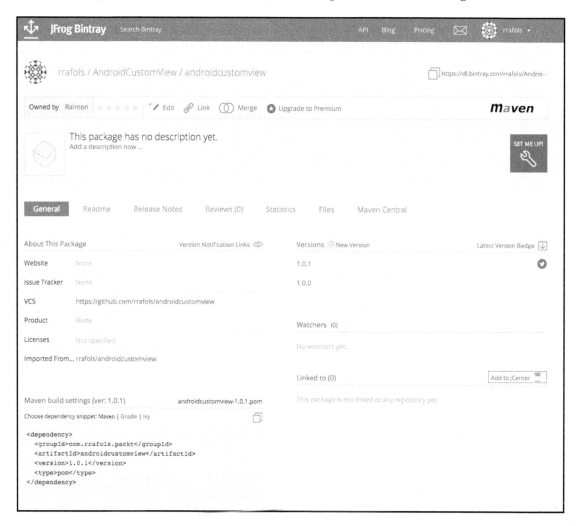

We can also inspect the files of an uploaded version to see what has been uploaded. If we go to a version and to the Files menu, we'll see the `.aar` Android library and all the other files the script has uploaded for us:

As we can see, it also packaged and uploaded the source code, the `Javadoc` and created a `.pom` file as it's hosted as a Maven repository.

After doing all these steps, we can upload it to `JCenter` directly from the artifact repository page by pressing **Add to JCenter**. Once approved, anyone wanting to use our library can simply define a dependency on `com.rrafols.packt.androidcustomview` and directly get it from `JCenter`.

For more information about this process and the author of these gradle build scripts, go to: `https://inthecheesefactory.com/blog/how-to-upload-library-to-jcenter-maven-central-as-dependency/en`.

Something we haven't mentioned but is also quite important is how to version our library. Whenever we're creating a new release, we create a version number. It is highly recommended to use semantic versioning, `MAJOR.MINOR.PATCH`, when versioning our custom view. This way we can easily indicate if changes in one version are introducing incompatibilities or not. For instance, using semantic versioning, if we change the major number, we're indicating we've introduced incompatibilities with previous versions, or by changing the minor number, we indicate we've added new functionality without introducing any incompatibility. This is important for third-parties or other developers using our library, so they know what to expect from one version to the next.

For more information on Semantic Versioning, go to: `http://semver.org/`.

Check also the full source code of this example in the `Example32-Library` folder on the GitHub repository.

Summary

In this chapter, we have seen the recommendations for sharing our custom view and how we can actually do it. There are many benefits from open sourcing our custom views or sharing them internally at our company, for example. We'll not only pay more attention to quality and to details, but we will also foster collaborations and enrich the Android developer community.

In the next chapters, we will see how we can put all the information we have been covering these last chapters and build some more complex custom views that we can use and include directly in our applications.

Implementing Your Own EPG

9

So far, we have been building very basic examples to show some of the functionalities and methods that Android provides us with to implement and draw our custom views. In this chapter, we will see a more complex example of a custom view. We'll be building an **Electronic Programming Guide** (**EPG**).

An EPG is a fairly complex component to build, and if done wrong, can have an impact on the user experience. For example, if it doesn't perform well, it'll feel sluggish and tedious to use.

We'll be using several things we have covered in previous chapters. All together it can be a bit too much, but we will be building it step by step, and, in more detail, we will cover:

- How to build a basic EPG custom view
- How to add basic animations and interactions
- How to allow zooming
- Making it configurable

Building an EPG

If we want to make our EPG useful, it should show several channels, and both current and future TV programs at the same time. Also, it'd be nice to clearly see what's currently playing, and have clear indicators of when other TV programs start and end.

In this specific component, we will opt for one method of rendering that covers these points. You can use it as an example, but there are many other ways to render the same kind of information. Also, it won't be connected to a backend service providing the EPG data. All EPG data will be mocked up, but it can be easily connected to any service, although some changes might need to be done.

EPG basics and animation setup

We'll start by creating a class-extending view. On its `onDraw()` method we will draw the following parts:

- The view background
- The EPG body with all the channels and TV programs
- A top time bar hinting at the time
- A vertical line indicating the current time

We'll also need to trigger a redraw cycle if we are animating some variables.

So, let's start with this implementation of the `onDraw()` method, and let's proceed method by method:

```
@Override
protected void onDraw(Canvas canvas) {
    animateLogic();

    long currentTime = System.currentTimeMillis();

    drawBackground(canvas);
    drawEPGBody(canvas, currentTime, frScrollY);
    drawTimeBar(canvas, currentTime);
    drawCurrentTime(canvas, currentTime);

    if (missingAnimations()) invalidate();
}
```

The easiest method to implement will be `drawBackground()`:

```
private static final int BACKGROUND_COLOR = 0xFF333333;
private void drawBackground(Canvas canvas) {
    canvas.drawARGB(BACKGROUND_COLOR >> 24,
            (BACKGROUND_COLOR >> 16) & 0xff,
            (BACKGROUND_COLOR >> 8) & 0xff,
            BACKGROUND_COLOR & 0xff);
}
```

In this case, we have defined a background color as `0xFF333333`, which is some kind of dark gray, and we are just filling the whole screen with the `drawARGB()` call, masking and shifting the color components.

Now, let's go for the `drawTimeBar()` method:

```
private void drawTimeBar(Canvas canvas, long currentTime) {
    calendar.setTimeInMillis(initialTimeValue - 120 * 60 * 1000);
    calendar.set(Calendar.MINUTE, 0);
    calendar.set(Calendar.SECOND, 0);
    calendar.set(Calendar.MILLISECOND, 0);

    long time = calendar.getTimeInMillis();
    float x = getTimeHorizontalPosition(time) - frScrollX + getWidth()
            / 4.f;

    while (x < getWidth()) {
        if (x > 0) {
            canvas.drawLine(x, 0, x, timebarHeight, paintTimeBar);
        }

        if (x + timeBarTextBoundaries.width() > 0) {
            SimpleDateFormat dateFormatter =
                    new SimpleDateFormat("HH:mm", Locale.US);

            String date = dateFormatter.format(new Date(time));
            canvas.drawText(date,
                    x + programMargin,
                    (timebarHeight - timeBarTextBoundaries.height()) /
                    2.f + timeBarTextBoundaries.height(),paintTimeBar);
        }

        time += 30 * 60 * 1000;
        x = getTimeHorizontalPosition(time) - frScrollX + getWidth() /
            4.f;
    }

    canvas.drawLine(0,
            timebarHeight,
            getWidth(),
            timebarHeight,
            paintTimeBar);
}
```

Let's explain what this method is doing:

1. First, we got the initial time at which we'd like to start drawing the time marks:

```
calendar.setTimeInMillis(initialTimeValue - 120 * 60 * 1000);
calendar.set(Calendar.MINUTE, 0);
calendar.set(Calendar.SECOND, 0);
calendar.set(Calendar.MILLISECOND, 0);

long time = calendar.getTimeInMillis();
```

We defined the `initialTimeValue` in our class constructor as half an hour to the current time. We also removed the minutes, seconds, and milliseconds as we'd like to indicate the exact hours and the exact half hour past each hour, for instance: 9.00, 9.30, 10.00, 10.30, and so on in this example.

Then we created a helper method to get the screen position based on a timestamp that will be used in many other places in the code:

```
private float getTimeHorizontalPosition(long ts) {
    long timeDifference = (ts - initialTimeValue);
    return timeDifference * timeScale;
}
```

2. In addition, we need to calculate a timescale based on the device screen density. To calculate it, we defined a default timescale:

```
private static final float DEFAULT_TIME_SCALE = 0.0001f;
```

3. In the class constructor, we adjusted the timescale depending on the screen density:

```
final float screenDensity =
getResources().getDisplayMetrics().density;
timeScale = DEFAULT_TIME_SCALE * screenDensity;
```

We know there are many Android devices with different screen sizes and densities. Doing it this way, instead of hardcoding the pixel dimensions, makes the rendering as close as possible on all devices.

With the help of this method, we can easily loop on blocks of half an hour until we reach the end of the screen:

```
float x = getTimeHorizontalPosition(time) - frScrollX + getWidth() / 4.f;
while (x < getWidth()) {

    ...
    time += 30 * 60 * 1000; // 30 minutes
    x = getTimeHorizontalPosition(time) - frScrollX + getWidth() / 4.f;
}
```

By adding 30 minutes, converted to milliseconds, to the time variable we increment the horizontal marks in blocks of 30 minutes.

We've taken into consideration the `frScrollX` position as well. This variable will be updated when we add interactions that allow us to scroll, but we will see that later in this chapter.

The rendering is quite straightforward: we draw a vertical line as long as the x coordinate is inside the screen:

```
if (x > 0) {
    canvas.drawLine(x, 0, x, timebarHeight, paintTimeBar);
}
```

we draw the time in HH:mm format, just next to it:

```
SimpleDateFormat dateFormatter = new SimpleDateFormat("HH:mm", Locale.US);
String date = dateFormatter.format(new Date(time));
canvas.drawText(date,
        x + programMargin,
        (timebarHeight - timeBarTextBoundaries.height()) / 2.f
                + timeBarTextBoundaries.height(), paintTimeBar);
```

One small performance improvement we can do is to store the strings so we don't have to call the format method again and again, and avoid costly object creation. We can do so by creating a **HashMap** that takes a long variable as a key and returns a string:

```
String date = null;
if (dateFormatted.containsKey(time)) {
    date = dateFormatted.get(time);
} else {
    date = dateFormatter.format(new Date(time));
    dateFormatted.put(time, date);
}
```

We use the formatted date if we already have it, or format it first and store it on the HashMap if it's the first time.

We can now go on to draw the current time indicator. It is quite easy; it's just a vertical box that is slightly wider than a single line, so we use `drawRect()` instead of `drawLine()`:

```
private void drawCurrentTime(Canvas canvas, long currentTime) {
    float currentTimePos = frChNameWidth +
    getTimeHorizontalPosition(currentTime) - frScrollX;
    canvas.drawRect(currentTimePos - programMargin/2,
            0,
            currentTimePos + programMargin/2,
            timebarHeight,
            paintCurrentTime);
    canvas.clipRect(frChNameWidth, 0, getWidth(), getHeight());
    canvas.drawRect(currentTimePos - programMargin/2,
            timebarHeight,
            currentTimePos + programMargin/2,
            getHeight(),
            paintCurrentTime);
}
```

As we already have the `getTimeHorizontalPosition` method, we can easily pinpoint where to draw the current time indicator. As we will be scrolling through the TV programs, we split the drawing into two parts: one that draws a line over the time bar, without any clipping; and another line from the end of the time bar to the bottom of the screen. In the latter we apply a clipping to only draw it on top of the TV programs.

To understand this more clearly, let's take a look at a screenshot of the result:

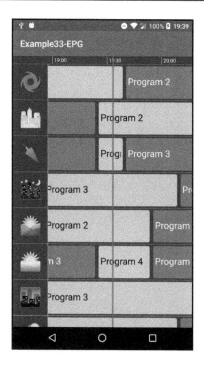

At the left side, we have got the icons representing the channels, on the top side is the time bar, and the rest is the body of the EPG with different TV programs. We'd like to avoid the current timeline, in red, going over the channel icons, so we apply the clipping we have just mentioned.

Finally, we can implement the drawing of the whole EPG body. It's a bit more complex than the other methods, so let's go through it step by step. First, we need to calculate the number of channels we have to draw to avoid doing unnecessary calculations and trying to draw outside the screen:

```
int startChannel = (int) (frScrollY / channelHeight);
verticalOffset -= startChannel * channelHeight;
int endChannel = startChannel + (int) ((getHeight() - timebarHeight) /
channelHeight) + 1;
if (endChannel >= channelList.length) endChannel = channelList.length - 1;
```

Like we did with the timescale, we also define a default channel height and compute it based on the screen density:

```
private static final int CHANNEL_HEIGHT = 80;
...
channelHeight = CHANNEL_HEIGHT * screenDensity;
```

Now that we know the initial channel and the end channel we need to draw, we can outline the drawing loop:

```
canvas.save();
canvas.clipRect(0, timebarHeight, getWidth(), getHeight());

for (int i = startChannel; i <= endChannel; i++) {
    float channelTop = (i - startChannel) * channelHeight -
    verticalOffset +
    timebarHeight;
    float channelBottom = channelTop + channelHeight;


    ...


}

canvas.drawLine(frChNameWidth, timebarHeight, frChNameWidth, getHeight(),
paintChannelText);
canvas.restore();
```

We'll be modifying the canvas clipping several times, so let's save it at the beginning of the method and restore it at the end. This way we won't impact any other drawing method completed after this. Inside the loop, for each channel, we also calculate the channelTop and channelBottom values as they'll be handy later when drawing it. These values indicate the vertical coordinates for the top and the bottom of the channel we are drawing.

Let's now draw the icon for each channel, requesting it first from the internet if we don't have it. We'll be using Picasso to manage the Internet requests, but we can use any other library:

```
if (channelList[i].getIcon() != null) {
    float iconMargin = (channelHeight -
    channelList[i].getIcon().getHeight()) / 2;

    canvas.drawBitmap(channelList[i].getIcon(), iconMargin, channelTop
    + iconMargin, null);

} else {
    if (channelTargets[i] == null) {
        channelTargets[i] = new ChannelIconTarget(channelList[i]);
```

```
        }

    Picasso.with(context)
            .load(channelList[i]
            .getIconUrl())
            .into(channelTargets[i]);
}
```

There is information about Picasso at:
`http://square.github.io/picasso/`.

Also, for each channel, we need to draw the TV programs that are inside the screen. Once again, let's use the method we previously created to convert a timestamp into a screen coordinate:

```
for (int j = 0; j < programs.size(); j++) {
    Program program = programs.get(j);

    long st = program.getStartTime();
    long et = program.getEndTime();

    float programStartX = getTimeHorizontalPosition(st);
    float programEndX = getTimeHorizontalPosition(et);

    if (programStartX - frScrollX > getWidth()) break;
    if (programEndX - frScrollX >= 0) {

        . . .

    }
}
```

Here, we are getting the program start and end positions from the program start and end times. If the start position is beyond the width of the screen, we can stop checking more TV programs as they'll all be outside the screen, assuming the TV programs are sorted by time in ascending order. Also, if the end position is less than 0, we can skip this specific TV program as it'll also be drawn outside the screen.

The actual drawing is quite simple; we are using a `drawRoundRect` for the TV program background and we are drawing the program name centered on it. We're also clipping the area just in case the name is longer than the TV program box:

```
canvas.drawRoundRect(horizontalOffset + programMargin + programStartX,
        channelTop + programMargin,
        horizontalOffset - programMargin + programEndX,
        channelBottom - programMargin,
        programMargin,
        programMargin,
```

```
            paintProgram);

canvas.save();
canvas.clipRect(horizontalOffset + programMargin * 2 + programStartX,
        channelTop + programMargin,
        horizontalOffset - programMargin * 2 + programEndX,
        channelBottom - programMargin);

paintProgramText.getTextBounds(program.getName(), 0,
program.getName().length(), textBoundaries);
float textPosition = channelTop + textBoundaries.height() + ((channelHeight
- programMargin * 2) - textBoundaries.height()) / 2;
canvas.drawText(program.getName(),
            horizontalOffset + programMargin * 2 + programStartX,
            textPosition,
            paintProgramText);
canvas.restore();
```

We've also added a small check to see if a TV program is currently playing. If the current time is greater than or equal to the program start time and smaller than its end time, we can conclude that the TV program is currently playing and render it with the highlighted color.

```
if (st <= currentTime && et > currentTime) {
    paintProgram.setColor(HIGHLIGHTED_PROGRAM_COLOR);
    paintProgramText.setColor(Color.BLACK);
} else {
    paintProgram.setColor(PROGRAM_COLOR);
    paintProgramText.setColor(Color.WHITE);
}
```

Let's now add the animation cycle. For this example, we have chosen the fixed time-step mechanism. We'll only animate the scroll variables, both horizontal and vertical, and the movement of the channel part of the screen:

```
private void animateLogic() {
    long currentTime = SystemClock.elapsedRealtime();
    accTime += currentTime - timeStart;
    timeStart = currentTime;

    while (accTime > TIME_THRESHOLD) {
        scrollX += (scrollXTarget - scrollX) / 4.f;
        scrollY += (scrollYTarget - scrollY) / 4.f;
        chNameWidth += (chNameWidthTarget - chNameWidth) / 4.f;
        accTime -= TIME_THRESHOLD;
    }

    float factor = ((float) accTime) / TIME_THRESHOLD;
    float nextScrollX = scrollX + (scrollXTarget - scrollX) / 4.f;
```

```
    float nextScrollY = scrollY + (scrollYTarget - scrollY) / 4.f;
    float nextChNameWidth = chNameWidth + (chNameWidthTarget -
                         chNameWidth) / 4.f;

    frScrollX = scrollX * (1.f - factor) + nextScrollX * factor;
    frScrollY = scrollY * (1.f - factor) + nextScrollY * factor;
    frChNameWidth = chNameWidth * (1.f - factor) + nextChNameWidth *
    factor;
}
```

In our renderings and calculations later, we will use the `frScrollX`, `frScrollY`, and `frChNameWidth` variables, which contain the fractional parts between the current logic tick and the following one.

We'll see how to scroll in the next section when talking about adding interaction to the EPG, but we have just introduced the movement of the channel part. Right now, we are only rendering each channel as an icon, but, to have more information, we have added a toggle that makes the channel box, where we currently have the icon, become larger and draw the channel title next to the icon.

We've created a Boolean switch to track which state we are rendering and to draw the channel name if required:

```
if (!shortChannelMode) {
    paintChannelText.getTextBounds(channelList[i].getName(),
            0,
            channelList[i].getName().length(),
            textBoundaries);

    canvas.drawText(channelList[i].getName(),
            channelHeight - programMargin * 2,
            (channelHeight - textBoundaries.height()) / 2 +
             textBoundaries.height() + channelTop,
            paintChannelText);
}
```

The toggle is quite simple, as it just changes the channel box width target to `channelHeight`, so it'll have square dimensions, or two times the `channelHeight` when drawing the text. The animation cycle will take care of animating the variable:

```
if (shortChannelMode) {
    chNameWidthTarget = channelHeight * 2;
    shortChannelMode = false;
} else {
    chNameWidthTarget = channelHeight;
    shortChannelMode = true;
}
```

Interaction

So far, it's not really useful as we can't interact with it. To add interaction, we need to override the `onTouchEvent()` method from the View, as we have seen in previous chapters.

In our own implementation of onTouchEvent, we are mainly interested in the `ACTION_DOWN`, `ACTION_UP,` and `ACTION_MOVE` events. Let's see the implementation we have done:

```
private float dragX;
private float dragY;
private boolean dragged;

...

@Override
public boolean onTouchEvent(MotionEvent event) {

    switch(event.getAction()) {
        case MotionEvent.ACTION_DOWN:
            dragX = event.getX();
            dragY = event.getY();

            getParent().requestDisallowInterceptTouchEvent(true);
            dragged = false;
            return true;

        case MotionEvent.ACTION_UP:
            if (!dragged) {
                // touching inside the channel area, will toggle
                    large/short channels
                if (event.getX() < frChNameWidth) {
                    switchNameWidth = true;
                    invalidate();
                }
            }

            getParent().requestDisallowInterceptTouchEvent(false);
            return true;

        case MotionEvent.ACTION_MOVE:
            float newX = event.getX();
            float newY = event.getY();

            scrollScreen(dragX - newX, dragY - newY);
```

```
                dragX = newX;
                dragY = newY;
                dragged = true;
                return true;
            default:
                return false;
        }
    }
```

This method doesn't contain that much logic; it's just checking if we are dragging on the screen, calling `scrollScreen` with the drag amount delta from the last event, and, in the case where we haven't dragged and just pressed on the channel box, triggering the toggle to make the channel box bigger or smaller.

The `scrollScreen` method simply updates the `scrollXTarget` and `scrollYTarget` and checks its boundaries:

```
    private void scrollScreen(float dx, float dy) {
        scrollXTarget += dx;
        scrollYTarget += dy;

        if (scrollXTarget < -chNameWidth) scrollXTarget = -chNameWidth;
        if (scrollYTarget < 0) scrollYTarget = 0;

        float maxHeight = channelList.length * channelHeight - getHeight()
        + 1 + timebarHeight;
        if (scrollYTarget > maxHeight) scrollYTarget = maxHeight;

        invalidate();
    }
```

Also, it's highly important to call `invalidate` to trigger a redraw event. On the `onDraw()` event itself, we check if all animations are finished and trigger more redraw events if needed:

```
    if (missingAnimations()) invalidate();
```

The actual implementation of `missingAnimations` is quite straightforward:

```
    private static final float ANIM_THRESHOLD = 0.01f;

    private boolean missingAnimations() {
        if (Math.abs(scrollXTarget - scrollX) > ANIM_THRESHOLD)
        return true;

    if (Math.abs(scrollYTarget - scrollY) > ANIM_THRESHOLD)
        return true;
```

```
if (Math.abs(chNameWidthTarget - chNameWidth) > ANIM_THRESHOLD)
    return true;

return false;
}
```

We're just checking all properties that can be animated if their difference from their target value is smaller than a predefined threshold. If only one is bigger than this threshold, we need to trigger more redraw events and animation cycles.

Zooming

As we are rendering a box for each TV program and its size is directly determined by the TV program duration, it might happen that TV program titles will be larger than its rendered box. In those cases, we might want to read some more parts of the title, or, at other times, we may like to compress things a bit so we can have an overall picture of what will be on TV later that day.

To solve this, we can implement a zooming mechanism by pinching on our device screen on top of our EPG widget. We can apply this zooming directly to the timeScale variable, and, as we have used it everywhere for all calculations, it'll keep everything synchronized:

```
scaleDetector = new ScaleGestureDetector(context,
    new ScaleGestureDetector.SimpleOnScaleGestureListener() {

    ...
    });
```

To simplify it, let's use the SimpleOnScaleGestureListener, which allows us to override only the methods we'd like to use.

Now, we need to modify the onTouchEvent to let the scaleDetector instance process the event as well:

```
@Override
public boolean onTouchEvent(MotionEvent event) {
    scaleDetector.onTouchEvent(event);

    if (zooming) {
        zooming = false;
        return true;
    }
```

```
        . . .
    }
```

We've also added a check to see if we are zooming. We'll update this variable in the
`ScaleDetector` implementation, but the concept is to avoid scrolling the view, or
processing drag events, if we are already zooming.

Let's now implement the `ScaleDetector`:

```
scaleDetector = new ScaleGestureDetector(context, new
ScaleGestureDetector.SimpleOnScaleGestureListener() {
    private long focusTime;
    private float scrollCorrection = 0.f;
    @Override
    public boolean onScaleBegin(ScaleGestureDetector detector) {
        zooming = true;
        focusTime = getHorizontalPositionTime(scrollXTarget +
        detector.getFocusX() - frChNameWidth);
        scrollCorrection = getTimeHorizontalPosition((focusTime)) -
        scrollXTarget;
        return true;
    }

    public boolean onScale(ScaleGestureDetector detector) {
        timeScale *= detector.getScaleFactor();
        timeScale = Math.max(DEFAULT_TIME_SCALE * screenDensity / 2,
                    Math.min(timeScale, DEFAULT_TIME_SCALE *
                    screenDensity * 4));

        // correct scroll position otherwise will move too much when
            zooming
        float current = getTimeHorizontalPosition((focusTime)) -
        scrollXTarget;
        float scrollDifference = current - scrollCorrection;
        scrollXTarget += scrollDifference;
        zooming = true;

        invalidate();
        return true;
    }

    @Override
    public void onScaleEnd(ScaleGestureDetector detector) {
        zooming = true;
    }
});
```

We're basically doing two different things. First, we adjust the `timeScale` variable from half the default value to four times the default value:

```
timeScale *= detector.getScaleFactor();
timeScale = Math.max(DEFAULT_TIME_SCALE * screenDensity / 2,
            Math.min(timeScale, DEFAULT_TIME_SCALE * screenDensity
            * 4));
```

Also, we adjust the scroll position to avoid an unpleasant effect when scaling. By adjusting the scroll position, we are trying to keep the focus of the pinch at the same position, even after zooming in or out.

```
float current = getTimeHorizontalPosition((focusTime)) - scrollXTarget;
float scrollDifference = current - scrollCorrection;
scrollXTarget += scrollDifference;
```

For more information about the `ScaleDetector` and gestures, check out the official Android documentation.

Configurations and Extensions

If want to create a custom view that is usable by many people, it needs to be customizable. The EPG is no exception. In our initial implementation, we hardcoded some colors and values, but let's see how we can extend these functionalities and make our EPG customizable.

Making it configurable

In the initial chapters of this book, we introduced how to add parameters and, that way, easily customize our custom view. Following the same principles, we have created an `attrs.xml` file with all the customizable parameters:

```xml
<?xml version="1.0" encoding="utf-8"?>
<resources>
    <declare-styleable name="EPG">
        <attr name="backgroundColor" format="color"/>
        <attr name="programColor" format="color"/>
        <attr name="highlightedProgramColor" format="color"/>
        <attr name="currentTimeColor" format="color"/>
        <attr name="channelTextColor" format="color"/>
        <attr name="programTextColor" format="color"/>
        <attr name="highlightedProgramTextColor" format="color"/>
```

```
        <attr name="timeBarColor" format="color"/>

        <attr name="channelHeight" format="float"/>
        <attr name="programMargin" format="float"/>
        <attr name="timebarHeight" format="float"/>
    </declare-styleable>
</resources>
```

There are many other variables that could be added as parameters, but these are the main customizations from the point of view of the custom view look and feel.

Also, in our class constructor, we have added the code to read and parse these parameters. In a case where they're not present, we'd default to the previous values we hardcoded.

```
TypedArray ta = context.getTheme().obtainStyledAttributes(attrs,
R.styleable.EPG, 0, 0);
try {
    backgroundColor = ta.getColor(R.styleable.EPG_backgroundColor,
    BACKGROUND_COLOR);
    paintChannelText.setColor(ta.getColor(R.styleable.EPG_channelTextColor
                    Color.WHITE));
    paintCurrentTime.setColor(ta.getColor(R.styleable.EPG_currentTimeColor,
                    CURRENT_TIME_COLOR));
    paintTimeBar.setColor(ta.getColor(R.styleable.EPG_timeBarColor,
                    Color.WHITE));

    highlightedProgramColor =
    ta.getColor(R.styleable.EPG_highlightedProgramColor,
        HIGHLIGHTED_PROGRAM_COLOR);

    programColor = ta.getColor(R.styleable.EPG_programColor,
    PROGRAM_COLOR);

    channelHeight = ta.getFloat(R.styleable.EPG_channelHeight,
    CHANNEL_HEIGHT) * screenDensity;

    programMargin = ta.getFloat(R.styleable.EPG_programMargin,
    PROGRAM_MARGIN) * screenDensity;

    timebarHeight = ta.getFloat(R.styleable.EPG_timebarHeight,
    TIMEBAR_HEIGHT) * screenDensity;

    programTextColor = ta.getColor(R.styleable.EPG_programTextColor,
    Color.WHITE);

    highlightedProgramTextColor =
    ta.getColor(R.styleable.EPG_highlightedProgramTextColor,
```

```
            Color.BLACK);
    } finally {
        ta.recycle();
    }
```

To make it simpler and clearer for anyone trying to customize it, we can do a small change. Let's redefine the parameters that map directly to pixel sizes as dimensions instead of floats:

```
<attr name="channelHeight" format="dimension"/>
<attr name="programMargin" format="dimension"/>
<attr name="timebarHeight" format="dimension"/>
```

Update the parsing code to the following:

```
channelHeight = ta.getDimension(R.styleable.EPG_channelHeight,
        CHANNEL_HEIGHT * screenDensity);

programMargin = ta.getDimension(R.styleable.EPG_programMargin,
        PROGRAM_MARGIN * screenDensity);

timebarHeight = ta.getDimension(R.styleable.EPG_timebarHeight,
        TIMEBAR_HEIGHT * screenDensity);
```

By using getDimension instead of getFloat, it'll automatically convert dimensions set as density pixels to actual pixels. It'll not do that transformation to the default value, so we still need to do the multiplication by the screenDensity ourselves.

Finally, we need to add these configurations in the activity_main.xml layout file:

```
<?xml version="1.0" encoding="utf-8"?>
<LinearLayout xmlns:android="http://schemas.android.com/apk/res/android"
    xmlns:tools="http://schemas.android.com/tools"
    android:layout_width="match_parent"
    android:layout_height="match_parent"
xmlns:app="http://schemas.android.com/apk/res-auto"
tools:context="com.rrafols.packt.epg.MainActivity">

    <com.rrafols.packt.epg.EPG
        android:id="@+id/epg_view"
        android:layout_width="match_parent"
        android:layout_height="match_parent"
        app:channelHeight="80dp"
        app:highlightedProgramColor="#ffffdd20"
        app:highlightedProgramTextColor="#ff000000"/>
</LinearLayout>
```

We can see the result of these changes in the following screenshot:

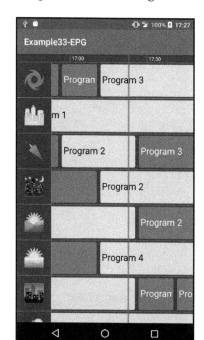

Implementing callbacks

Another critical functionality from our EPG that we haven't covered yet is the ability to actually do something when clicking on a TV program. If we want to do something useful with our EPG, rather than just showing the titles of what is coming, we must implement this functionality.

This implementation is quite straightforward and will handle the logic to an external listener or callback. It would also be quite easy to modify the source code to implement some custom behavior on the EPG itself.

To begin, we create a new interface inside the EPG class with one single method:

```
interface EPGCallback {
    void programClicked(Channel channel, Program program);
}
```

This method will be called whenever we click on a TV program, and whoever is implementing this callback will get both the `Channel` and the TV `Program`.

Now, let's modify the `onTouchEvent()` method to handle this new functionality:

```
if (event.getX() < frChNameWidth) {

    ...
} else {
    clickProgram(event.getX(), event.getY());
}
```

In our previous code, we were checking only if we clicked on the channel area of the screen. Now we can use the other area to detect if we have clicked inside a TV program.

Let's now implement the `clickProgram()` method:

```
private void clickProgram(float x, float y) {
    long ts = getHorizontalPositionTime(scrollXTarget + x -
    frChNameWidth);
    int channel = (int) ((y + frScrollY - timebarHeight) /
    channelHeight);

    ArrayList<Program> programs = channelList[channel].getPrograms();
    for (int i = 0; i < programs.size(); i++) {
        Program pr = programs.get(i);
        if (ts >= pr.getStartTime() && ts < pr.getEndTime()) {
            if (callback != null) {
                callback.programClicked(channelList[channel], pr);
            }
            break;
        }
    }
}
```

We first convert the horizontal position where the user clicks into a timestamp, and, with the vertical position of the touch event, we can determine the channel. With the channel and the timestamp, we could check which program the user has clicked inside and call the callback with that information.

In the GitHub example, we added a dummy listener that will only log the channel and program clicked:

```
@Override
protected void onCreate(Bundle savedInstanceState) {
    super.onCreate(savedInstanceState);
    setContentView(R.layout.activity_main);

    EPG epg = (EPG) findViewById(R.id.epg_view);
    epg.setCallback(new EPG.EPGCallback() {
        @Override
        public void programClicked(Channel channel, Program program) {
            Log.d("EPG", "program clicked: " + program.getName() + "
            channel: " + channel.getName());
        }
    });

    populateDummyChannelList(epg);
}
```

There is also a `populateDummyChannelList()` method in this Activity `onCreate`. This method will only populate random channel and TV program data and should be removed if connecting with a real EPG data provider.

The whole example can be found in the `Example33-EPG` folder on the GitHub repository.

Summary

In this chapter, we have seen how to build a simple EPG with many functionalities, but we have probably left many others without an implementation. For instance, our TV program rendering is rather simple, and we could add way more information inside the TV program box, such as the duration, start time, and end time, or even show the TV program description directly there.

Feel free to take what's in the GitHub repository and play with it, add new customizations or functionalities, and adapt it to your needs.

We haven't specifically talked about performance that much, but we have tried to minimize the amount of allocations inside our `onDraw` method and the methods called by it as much as possible, and we have reduced what we are drawing on the screen as much as possible and don't even process elements that will fall outside the screen boundaries.

Taking into account these details is critical if we want our custom view, or the EPG in this case, to be snappy, responsive, and scale with more channels and TV programs.

In the next chapter we will be building another complex custom view that we can use to draw graphs on our Android applications.

10
Building a Charts Component

In the previous chapter, we saw how to build a complex custom view that combined a bit of everything we've covered in this book. It included some rendering code, used a third-party library, had touch interactions and animations, and we briefly talked about performance considerations. It was a rather complete custom view example, but it's not the only one. In this chapter, we'll be building another complex custom view. Step by step, we'll build a charts custom view to draw graphs we can embed in our Android applications. We'll start by building a very basic implementation and we'll be adding additional features and functionalities along the way. In more detail, we'll see about:

- Building a basic charts component
- How to take into account margins and padding
- Using Paths to improve rendering
- Updating and growing our data set
- Rendering additional features and customizations

Building a basic chart custom view

Most probably, at one point or another, we'll have to draw some charts in an Android application. It can be a static chart, which isn't that fun as it can be replaced simply by an image, or it can be a dynamic chart, allowing user interactions and reactions to data changes. This last case is where we can use a custom view to draw real-time graphs, add multiple sources of data, and even animate it. Let's start by building a very simple custom view where we'll add more features later on.

Margins and padding

As with any normal view, our custom view will be subject to the layout manager's margins and to the view's padding. We should not worry that much about the margin values, as the layout manager will directly process them and will transparently modify the size available for our custom view. The values we've to take into consideration are the padding values. As we can see in the following image, the margin is the space the layout manager is adding before and after our custom view and the padding is the internal space between the view boundaries and the content itself:

Our view has to manage this padding appropriately. To do so, we can directly use the different `getPadding` methods from `canvas` such as `getPaddingTop()`, `getPaddingBottom()`, `getPaddingStart()`, and so on. Using the padding values, we should adjust the rendering area accordingly on our `onDraw()` method:

```
protected void onDraw(Canvas canvas) {
    int startPadding = getPaddingStart();
    int topPadding = getPaddingTop();

    int width = canvas.getWidth() - startPadding - getPaddingEnd();
    int height = canvas.getHeight() - topPadding - getPaddingBottom();
}
```

In this code, we're storing the left and topmost points of our `Canvas` which are the start and top padding values respectively. We have to be careful with this sentence as the start padding might not be the left padding. If we check the documentation we'll find there are both `getPaddingStart()`, `getPaddingEnd()`, `getPaddingLeft()`, and `getPaddingRight()`. The start padding, for example, can be the right padding if our device is configured in **Right-To-Left** (**RTL**) mode. We have to be careful with these details if we'd like to support both LTR and RTL devices. In this specific example, we'll build it with RTL support by detecting the layout direction using the `getLayoutDirection()` method available on view. But first, let's focus on a very simple implementation.

Basic implementation

Our basic implementation will be quite straightforward. Let's start by creating the class and its constructor:

```
public class Chart extends View {
    private Paint linePaint;

    public Chart(Context context, AttributeSet attrs) {
        super(context, attrs);
        linePaint = new Paint();
        linePaint.setAntiAlias(true);
        linePaint.setColor(0xffffffff);
        linePaint.setStrokeWidth(8.f);
        linePaint.setStyle(Paint.Style.STROKE);
    }
}
```

We've initialized a `Paint` object on our constructor, but this time we've set the style to `Paint.Style.STROKE` as we're only interested in drawing lines. Let's now add a method so whoever is using the custom view can set the data to render:

```
private float[] dataPoints;
private float minValue;
private float maxValue;
private float verticalDelta;

public void setDataPoints(float[] originalData) {
    dataPoints = new float[originalData.length];
    minValue = Float.MAX_VALUE;
    maxValue = Float.MIN_VALUE;
    for (int i = 0; i< dataPoints.length; i++) {
        dataPoints[i] = originalData[i];
        if (dataPoints[i] <minValue) minValue = dataPoints[i];
        if (dataPoints[i] >maxValue) maxValue = dataPoints[i];
    }

    verticalDelta = maxValue - minValue;
    postInvalidate();
}
```

We're making a copy of the original data array as we don't have control over it and it might change without prior warning. Later, we'll see how can we improve this behavior and adapt to changes to the data set.

We're also calculating the maximum and minimum values on the array and the difference between them. This will allow us to get a relative scale of those numbers and scale them down, or up if needed, to a 0 to 1 scale, which will be quite handy for adjusting the rendering to our view height.

Now that we have the data, we can implement our onDraw() method:

```
@Override
protected void onDraw(Canvas canvas) {
    canvas.drawARGB(255,0 ,0 ,0);
    float leftPadding = getPaddingLeft();
    float topPadding = getPaddingTop();

    float width = canvas.getWidth() - leftPadding - getPaddingRight();
    float height = canvas.getHeight() - topPadding -
    getPaddingBottom();

    float lastX = getPaddingStart();
    float lastY = height * ((dataPoints[0] - minValue) / verticalDelta)
    + topPadding;
    for (int i = 1; i < dataPoints.length; i++) {
        float y = height * ((dataPoints[i] - minValue) / verticalDelta)
        + topPadding;
        float x = width * (((float) i + 1) / dataPoints.length) +
        leftPadding;

        canvas.drawLine(lastX, lastY, x, y, linePaint);
        lastX = x;
        lastY = y;
    }
}
```

To keep it as simple as possible, for the time being, we're drawing a black background with canvas.drawARGB(255, 0, 0, 0) and then we're computing the available size on our Canvas by subtracting the paddings from the total width and height.

We're also splitting the horizontal space equally for all the points and scaling them vertically to use the whole available space. As we've calculated the difference between the minimum and maximum value of our data set, we can scale those numbers to a 0 to 1 range by subtracting the minimum value of the number and then dividing by the difference or verticalDelta as the variable we're using here.

With these calculations, we only have to keep track of the previous values in order to be able to draw a line from the old point to the new one. Here, we are storing the last x and y coordinates in the lastX and lastY variables respectively and we are updating them at the end of every single loop.

Optimizations and improvements with Paths

We could actually pre-calculate these operations we're doing on the onDraw() method as there is no need to do it every single time we're drawing the chart on the screen. We could just do it at the setDataPoints(), which is the only point in our custom view that our data set can be changed or replaced:

```
public void setDataPoints(float[] originalData) {
    dataPoints = new float[originalData.length];

    float minValue = Float.MAX_VALUE;
    float maxValue = Float.MIN_VALUE;
    for (int i = 0; i < dataPoints.length; i++) {
        dataPoints[i] = originalData[i];
        if (dataPoints[i] < minValue) minValue = dataPoints[i];
        if (dataPoints[i] > maxValue) maxValue = dataPoints[i];
    }

    float verticalDelta = maxValue - minValue;

    for (int i = 0; i < dataPoints.length; i++) {
        dataPoints[i] = (dataPoints[i] - minValue) / verticalDelta;
    }

    postInvalidate();
}
```

Now, we can simplify our onDraw() method as we can safely assume our data set will always range between 0 and 1:

```
@Override
protected void onDraw(Canvas canvas) {
    canvas.drawARGB(255,0 ,0 ,0);
    float leftPadding = getPaddingLeft();
    float topPadding = getPaddingTop();

    float width = canvas.getWidth() - leftPadding - getPaddingRight();
    float height = canvas.getHeight() - topPadding -
    getPaddingBottom();
```

```
        float lastX = getPaddingStart();
        float lastY = height * dataPoints[0] + topPadding;
        for (int i = 1; i < dataPoints.length; i++) {
            float y = height * dataPoints[i] + topPadding;
            float x = width * (((float) i) / dataPoints.length) +
            leftPadding;

            canvas.drawLine(lastX, lastY, x, y, linePaint);

            lastX = x;
            lastY = y;
        }
    }
```

But we can go further and convert the line drawings into a Path:

```
    private Path graphPath;

    @Override
    protected void onDraw(Canvas canvas) {
        canvas.drawARGB(255,0 ,0 ,0);

        float leftPadding = getPaddingLeft();
        float topPadding = getPaddingTop();

        float width = canvas.getWidth() - leftPadding - getPaddingRight();
        float height = canvas.getHeight() - topPadding -
        getPaddingBottom();

        if (graphPath == null) {
            graphPath = new Path();

            graphPath.moveTo(leftPadding, height * dataPoints[0] +
            topPadding);

            for (int i = 1; i < dataPoints.length; i++) {
                float y = height * dataPoints[i] + topPadding;
                float x = width * (((float) i + 1) / dataPoints.length) +
                leftPadding;

                graphPath.lineTo(x, y);
            }
        }

        canvas.drawPath(graphPath, linePaint);
    }
```

It will generate a `Path` with all the lines from one point to another the very first time the `onDraw()` method is called. The graph will be also scaled to the `canvas` dimensions. The only issue we will have now is that it'll not automatically adjust to a `canvas` size change or if our graph data is updated. Let's see how we can fix it.

First, we have to declare a `boolean` flag to determine if we've to regenerate the Path or not and two variables to hold the last width and height of our custom view:

```
private boolean regenerate;
private float lastWidth;
private float lastHeight;
```

In our class constructor, we have to create an instance of the `Path`. Later on, instead of checking with null and creating a new instance, we'd call the reset method to generate a new `Path`, but reusing this way the object instance:

```
graphPath = new Path();
lastWidth = -1;
lastHeight = -1;
```

On `setDataPoints()` we have to set `regenerate` to true just before the call to `postInvalidate`. And on our `onDraw()` method, we've to add additional checks to detect when the `canvas` size changes:

```
if (lastWidth != width || lastHeight != height) {
    regenerate = true;

    lastWidth = width;
    lastHeight = height;
}
```

As we have just mentioned, instead of checking with null, we will check the value of the `boolean` flag to regenerate the `Path`:

```
if (regenerate) {
    graphPath.reset();
    graphPath.moveTo(leftPadding, height * dataPoints[0] + topPadding);

    for (int i = 1; i < dataPoints.length; i++) {
        float y = height * dataPoints[i] + topPadding;
        float x = width * (((float) i + 1) / dataPoints.length) +
        leftPadding;

        graphPath.lineTo(x, y);
    }
```

```
        regenerate = false;
    }
```

Background lines and details

Let's add it into an Android project to see the results. First let's create a very simple layout file:

```xml
<?xml version="1.0" encoding="utf-8"?>
<LinearLayout xmlns:android="http://schemas.android.com/apk/res/android"
    xmlns:tools="http://schemas.android.com/tools"
    android:layout_width="match_parent"
    android:layout_height="match_parent"
    xmlns:app="http://schemas.android.com/apk/res-auto"
    tools:context="com.rrafols.packt.chart.MainActivity">

    <com.rrafols.packt.chart.Chart
        android:layout_margin="16dp"
        android:padding="10dp"
        android:id="@+id/chart_view"
        android:layout_width="match_parent"
        android:layout_height="match_parent" />

</LinearLayout>
```

Let's also create an empty activity that will only set this layout file as the content View and generate some random data for our chart component to render:

```java
@Override
protected void onCreate(Bundle savedInstanceState) {
    super.onCreate(savedInstanceState);
    setContentView(R.layout.activity_main);

    Chart chart = (Chart) findViewById(R.id.chart_view);

    float[] data = new float[20];
    for (int i = 0; i < data.length; i++) {
        data[i] = (float) Math.random() * 10.f;
    }

    chart.setDataPoints(data);
}
```

If we run this example, we'll get the following screen:

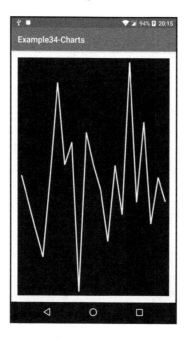

OK, we've a simple implementation done, but let's add some details. We'll start by adding a small dot on each data point for improved clarity. Let's create a new `Paint` object on our class constructor for that:

```
circlePaint = new Paint();
circlePaint.setAntiAlias(true);
circlePaint.setColor(0xffff2020);
circlePaint.setStyle(Paint.Style.FILL);
```

Now, one approach to do so, is to create an additional Path that will draw small circles on each data point. Using the same approach as we did for the line Path, we'll create an instance of the `circlePath` on the class constructor and reset it whenever it has to be regenerated. As we're calculating the coordinates for the lines, we can reuse them as the location of the circles:

```
@Override
protected void onDraw(Canvas canvas) {
    canvas.drawARGB(255,0 ,0 ,0);

    float leftPadding = getPaddingLeft();
    float topPadding = getPaddingTop();
```

```
    float width = canvas.getWidth() - leftPadding - getPaddingRight();
    float height = canvas.getHeight() - topPadding -
    getPaddingBottom();

    if (lastWidth != width || lastHeight != height) {

        regenerate = true;

        lastWidth = width;
        lastHeight = height;
    }

    if (regenerate) {
        circlePath.reset();
        graphPath.reset();

        float x = leftPadding;
        float y = height * dataPoints[0] + topPadding;

        graphPath.moveTo(x, y);
        circlePath.addCircle(x, y, 10, Path.Direction.CW);

        for (int i = 1; i < dataPoints.length; i++) {
            y = height * dataPoints[i] + topPadding;
            x = width * (((float) i + 1) / dataPoints.length) +
            leftPadding;

            graphPath.lineTo(x, y);
            circlePath.addCircle(x, y, 10, Path.Direction.CW);
        }

        regenerate = false;
    }

    canvas.drawPath(graphPath, linePaint);
    canvas.drawPath(circlePath, circlePaint);
}
```

In this example, we've hard coded the radius of the circle to 10, just a bit bigger than the thickness of the lines: 8, but we'll talk about customizations later on this chapter.

If we now run this example, we'll see the difference from our previous version:

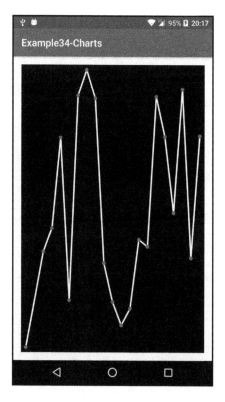

To add a more visual reference, let's also add some background lines. As it will be drawn using different settings, let's first create a new `Paint` object:

```
backgroundPaint = new Paint();
backgroundPaint.setColor(0xffBBBB40);
backgroundPaint.setStyle(Paint.Style.STROKE);
backgroundPaint.setPathEffect(new DashPathEffect(new float[] {5, 5}, 0));
```

Now, let's modify the `onDraw()` method to also generate a new `Path` with the background lines:

```
@Override
protected void onDraw(Canvas canvas) {
    canvas.drawARGB(255,0 ,0 ,0);

    float leftPadding = getPaddingLeft();
    float topPadding = getPaddingTop();
```

```
float width = canvas.getWidth() - leftPadding - getPaddingRight();
float height = canvas.getHeight() - topPadding -
getPaddingBottom();

if (lastWidth != width || lastHeight != height) {
    regenerate = true;

    lastWidth = width;
    lastHeight = height;
}

if (regenerate) {
    circlePath.reset();
    graphPath.reset();
    backgroundPath.reset();

    for (int i = 0; i <= dataPoints.length; i++) {
        float xl = width * (((float) i) / dataPoints.length) +
        leftPadding;
        backgroundPath.moveTo(xl, topPadding);
        backgroundPath.lineTo(xl, topPadding + height);
    }

    for (int i = 0; i <= 10; i++) {
        float yl = ((float) i / 10.f) * height + topPadding;
        backgroundPath.moveTo(leftPadding, yl);
        backgroundPath.lineTo(leftPadding + width, yl);
    }

    float x = leftPadding;
    float y = height * dataPoints[0] + topPadding;

    graphPath.moveTo(x, y);
    circlePath.addCircle(x, y, 10, Path.Direction.CW);

    for (int i = 1; i < dataPoints.length; i++) {
        x = width * (((float) i + 1) / dataPoints.length) +
        leftPadding;
        y = height * dataPoints[i] + topPadding;

        graphPath.lineTo(x, y);
        circlePath.addCircle(x, y, 10, Path.Direction.CW);
    }

    regenerate = false;
}

canvas.drawPath(backgroundPath, backgroundPaint);
```

```
        canvas.drawPath(graphPath, linePaint);
        canvas.drawPath(circlePath, circlePaint);
    }
```

Here, we are creating both horizontal and vertical lines. Horizontal lines will be created at the same exact points there will be a data point. We won't follow the same principle for vertical lines, we'll just draw 10 vertical lines uniformly separated between the top and the bottom of our `Canvas`. Executing our example now, we'll get something similar to the following screen:

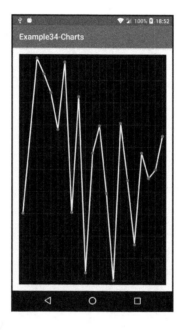

That's alright, but we are still missing some reference points. Let's draw some horizontal and vertical labels.

First, let's create an array of labels and create a method to let anyone using this custom view set them:

```
private String[] labels;

public void setLabels(String[] labels) {
    this.labels = labels;
}
```

If they're not set, we can either don't draw anything or generate them ourselves. In this example, we'll generate them ourselves automatically using the array index:

```
if (labels == null) {
    labels = new String[dataPoints.length + 1];
    for (int i = 0; i < labels.length; i++) {
        labels[i] = "" + i;
    }
}
```

To measure the text, so we can center it, we'll reuse a `Rect` object. Let's create and instantiate it:

```
private Rect textBoundaries = new Rect();
```

Now, we can add the following code to the `onDraw()` method to draw the bottom labels, one for each point in our data set:

```
for (int i = 0; i <= dataPoints.length; i++) {
    float xl = width * (((float) i) / dataPoints.length) + leftPadding;
    backgroundPaint.getTextBounds(labels[i], 0, labels[i].length(),
    textBoundaries);
    canvas.drawText(labels[i],
        xl - (textBoundaries.width() / 2),
        height + topPadding + backgroundPaint.getTextSize() * 1.5f,
        backgroundPaint);
}
```

We have also adjusted the total height of the graph to add some space for the labels:

```
float height = canvas.getHeight() - topPadding - getPaddingBottom()
        - backgroundPaint.getTextSize() + 0.5f;
```

Let's also draw a side legend indicating the value and scale of the points. As we're drawing a pre-defined set of vertical lines, we just have to calculate these values. We'd have to convert these values from the 0 to 1 range back to their original range and specific value.

We'd have to adjust the width and the initial left point of the graph depending on the label size. So, in addition, let's calculate the maximum width of the side labels:

```
float maxLabelWidth = 0.f;

for (int i = 0; i <= 10; i++) {
    float step = ((float) i / 10.f);
    float value = step * verticalDelta + minValue;
    verticalLabels[i] = decimalFormat.format(value);
    backgroundPaint.getTextBounds(verticalLabels[i], 0,
    verticalLabels[i].length(), textBoundaries);
```

```
    if (textBoundaries.width() > maxLabelWidth) {
        maxLabelWidth = textBoundaries.width();
    }
}
```

We also used a `DecimalFormat` instance to format the floating point values. We've created this `DecimalFormat` with the following pattern:

```
decimalFormat = new DecimalFormat("#.##");
```

In addition, we're storing the labels in an array to avoid regenerating them every single time we're drawing our view. With the maximum label width stored in the `maxLabelWidth` variable, we can adjust the paddings:

```
float labelLeftPadding = getPaddingLeft() + maxLabelWidth * 0.25f;
float leftPadding = getPaddingLeft() + maxLabelWidth * 1.5f;
```

We'll still use `leftPadding` to render all the objects and `labelLeftPadding` to render the labels. We have added the size of the maximum label and an additional *50%* of padding that will be distributed before and after the label when drawing it. For that reason, the labels will be rendered with an additional *25%* of `maxLabelWidth` padding, so there will be another *25%* of space between the end of the label and the start of the graph.

We can easily draw the vertical labels by just iterating the array and computing the right vertical position:

```
for (int i = 0; i <= 10; i++) {
    float step = ((float) i / 10.f);
    float yl = step * height + topPadding- (backgroundPaint.ascent() +
    backgroundPaint.descent()) * 0.5f;
    canvas.drawText(verticalLabels[i],
        labelLeftPadding,
        yl,
        backgroundPaint);
}
```

To center the text on a vertical coordinate, we're using the average between the ascent and descent from the current font.

If we now run this example, we'll have a more detailed view of our graph:

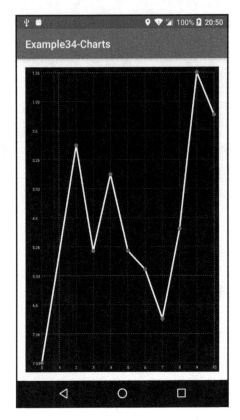

We said, early in this chapter, that we'll build support for RTL and LTR devices. In this graph view, the legend will feel more natural on the right side of the screen if the device layout is configured as RTL. Let's quickly implement this change:

```
float labelLeftPadding = getPaddingLeft() + maxLabelWidth * 0.25f;
float leftPadding = getPaddingLeft() + maxLabelWidth * 1.5f;
float rightPadding = getPaddingRight();
float topPadding = getPaddingTop();

float width = canvas.getWidth() - leftPadding - rightPadding;
float height = canvas.getHeight() - topPadding - getPaddingBottom()
        - backgroundPaint.getTextSize() + 0.5f;

if (getLayoutDirection() == LAYOUT_DIRECTION_RTL) {
    leftPadding = getPaddingEnd();
    labelLeftPadding = leftPadding + width + maxLabelWidth * 0.25f;
}
```

The only change we've to do is to is checking if the layout direction is
`LAYOUT_DIRECTION_RTL` and change the `leftPadding` and the `labelLeftPadding` to
update where to draw the graph and the labels.

Customizations

In the last chapter we've already seen how to add parameters to our custom view. On the
graph custom view we're building in this chapter, we could configure, for example, colors,
thickness of the lines, size of dots, and so on, but instead we'll focus on other kinds of
customizations, for example, inverting the vertical axis, and enabling or disabling the
rendering of the bottom and side labels or graph legend. Contrasting with the previous
configurations, these will require some additional code tweaks and specific
implementations.

Let's start by allowing inverting the vertical axis. Our default implementation will render
the smaller values on top and the bigger values at the bottom of our graph. This might not
be the expected result, so let's add a way to invert the axis:

```
private boolean invertVerticalAxis;

public void setInvertVerticalAxis(boolean invertVerticalAxis) {
    this.invertVerticalAxis = invertVerticalAxis;
    regenerate = true;
    postInvalidate();
}
```

Then, we have to change only how labels are generated and invert, if applicable, the values
of the data points. To change the generation of labels, we can do it by simply updating the
order of the steps. Instead of getting a number from 0 to 1, we'll invert the process and get a
number from 1 to 0:

```
float maxLabelWidth = 0.f;
if (regenerate) {
    for (int i = 0; i <= 10; i++) {
        float step;

        if (!invertVerticalAxis) {
            step = ((float) i / 10.f);
        } else {
            step = ((float) (10 - i)) / 10.f;
        }

        float value = step * verticalDelta + minValue;
        verticalLabels[i] = decimalFormat.format(value);
```

```
        backgroundPaint.getTextBounds(verticalLabels[i], 0,
        verticalLabels[i].length(), textBoundaries);
        if (textBoundaries.width() > maxLabelWidth) {
            maxLabelWidth = textBoundaries.width();
        }
    }
}
```

To get an inverted value of a data point, if needed, depending on the flag's value, let's add a new method to do so:

```
private float getDataPoint(int i) {
    float data = dataPoints[i];
    return invertVerticalAxis ? 1.f - data : data;
}
```

Now, instead of getting the data points directly from the array, we should use this method, as it will transparently invert the number if needed.

As we've mentioned before, we've also added a setLabels() method, so labels can also be externally customized.

We can also add a boolean flag to allow or prevent drawing the legend and background lines:

```
private boolean drawLegend;

public void setDrawLegend(boolean drawLegend) {
    this.drawLegend = drawLegend;
    regenerate = true;
    postInvalidate();
}
```

Simply check the status of this flag before drawing the background lines and labels.

See the full example in the Example34-Charts folder on the GitHub repository.

Adding advanced features

We've been building a simple implementation of a charts custom view. But we'll need some more features or our custom view might feel a bit static or not really useful. We can't build all the features we might think of or probably need. Also, we should be careful of not building a Swiss army knife custom view as it might become hard to maintain and might have an impact on the custom view performance.

Real-time updates

In our first plain implementation of our custom view, we've created a method to set the data points but we couldn't modify or update the data. Let's implement some quick changes to be able to dynamically add points. In this implementation, we adjusted the values to the 0 to 1 scale directly on the `setDataPoints()` method. As we'll provide a method to add new data values, we might get values outside the original minimum and maximum values, invalidating the scale we calculated before.

Let's first store the data in a collection instead of an array, so we can easily add new values:

```
private ArrayList<Float> dataPoints;

public void setDataPoints(float[] originalData) {
    ArrayList<Float> array = new ArrayList<>();
    for (float data : originalData) {
        array.add(data);
    }

    setDataPoints(array);
}

public void setDataPoints(ArrayList<Float> originalData) {
    dataPoints = new ArrayList<Float>();
    dataPoints.addAll(originalData);

    adjustDataRange();
}
```

We'll be storing the data in an `ArrayList` and we've modified the `setDataPoints()` method in order to be able to do so. Also, we have created the `adjustDataRange()` method to recalculate the range of the data and trigger a data regeneration and a redraw of our view:

```
private void adjustDataRange() {
    minValue = Float.MAX_VALUE;
    maxValue = Float.MIN_VALUE;
    for (int i = 0; i < dataPoints.size(); i++) {
        if (dataPoints.get(i) < minValue) minValue = dataPoints.get(i);
        if (dataPoints.get(i) > maxValue) maxValue = dataPoints.get(i);
    }

    verticalDelta = maxValue - minValue;

    regenerate = true;
```

```
        postInvalidate();
    }
```

The implementation of the addValue() method is quite simple. We add the new data to the ArrayList and if it's inside the current range, we just trigger a regeneration of the graph and a redraw of our view. If it's outside the current range, we call the adjustDataRange() method to adjust all the data to the new range:

```
public void addValue(float data) {
    dataPoints.add(data);

    if (data < minValue || data > maxValue) {
        adjustDataRange();
    } else {
        regenerate = true;
        postInvalidate();
    }
}
```

We just need to modify the getDataPoint() method to adjust the data to the 0 to 1 range:

```
private float getDataPoint(int i) {
    float data = (dataPoints.get(i) - minValue) / verticalDelta;
    return invertVerticalAxis ? 1.f - data : data;
}
```

If we run the example, we can see we can add new points to the graph and it will adjust automatically. To completely change or update the data, the method setDataPoints() must be called.

Multiple data sets

Sometimes, we'd like to show multiple graphs to compare them or simply to show multiple data sets at the same time. Let's do some modifications to allow two graphs at the same time in our graph custom view. It can be further extended to support even more graphs, but let's limit it to two to simplify the logic in this example.

First, we need to create different Paint and Path objects for each graph. We'll create arrays to store them as it'll be easier, later on, to iterate and render them. For example, we can create several Paint objects with different colors for each graph:

```
linePaint = new Paint[2];
linePaint[0] = new Paint();
linePaint[0].setAntiAlias(true);
linePaint[0].setColor(0xffffffff);
linePaint[0].setStrokeWidth(8.f);
linePaint[0].setStyle(Paint.Style.STROKE);

linePaint[1] = new Paint();
linePaint[1].setAntiAlias(true);
linePaint[1].setColor(0xff4040ff);
linePaint[1].setStrokeWidth(8.f);
linePaint[1].setStyle(Paint.Style.STROKE);
circlePaint = new Paint[2];
circlePaint[0] = new Paint();
circlePaint[0].setAntiAlias(true);
circlePaint[0].setColor(0xffff2020);
circlePaint[0].setStyle(Paint.Style.FILL);
circlePaint[1] = new Paint();
circlePaint[1].setAntiAlias(true);
circlePaint[1].setColor(0xff20ff20);
circlePaint[1].setStyle(Paint.Style.FILL);
```

Actually, it's a lot of work to set the same parameters again and again, so we can use another constructor from `Paint` that copies the attributes from an already existing `Paint` object:

```
linePaint = new Paint[2];
linePaint[0] = new Paint();
linePaint[0].setAntiAlias(true);
linePaint[0].setColor(0xffffffff);
linePaint[0].setStrokeWidth(8.f);
linePaint[0].setStyle(Paint.Style.STROKE);
linePaint[1] = new Paint(linePaint[0]);
linePaint[1].setColor(0xff4040ff);

circlePaint = new Paint[2];
circlePaint[0] = new Paint();
circlePaint[0].setAntiAlias(true);
circlePaint[0].setColor(0xffff2020);
circlePaint[0].setStyle(Paint.Style.FILL);

circlePaint[1] = new Paint(circlePaint[0]);
circlePaint[1].setColor(0xff20ff20);
```

Also, the `Path` objects and the data storage:

```
graphPath = new Path[2];
graphPath[0] = new Path();
graphPath[1] = new Path();

circlePath = new Path[2];
circlePath[0] = new Path();
circlePath[1] = new Path();

dataPoints = (ArrayList<Float>[]) new ArrayList[2];
```

We had also need a mechanism to add data to a specific data set:

```
public void setDataPoints(ArrayList<Float> originalData, int index) {
    dataPoints[index] = new ArrayList<Float>();
    dataPoints[index].addAll(originalData);

    adjustDataRange();
}
```

As we will have different data sets, we've to calculate the minimum and maximum values of all data sets. We will be using the same scale on each graph so it will be easier to compare:

```
private void adjustDataRange() {
    minValue = Float.MAX_VALUE;
    maxValue = Float.MIN_VALUE;
    for (int j = 0; j < dataPoints.length; j++) {
        for (int i = 0; dataPoints[j] != null && i <
        dataPoints[j].size(); i++) {
            if (dataPoints[j].get(i) < minValue) minValue =
            dataPoints[j].get(i);
            if (dataPoints[j].get(i) > maxValue) maxValue =
            dataPoints[j].get(i);
        }
    }

    verticalDelta = maxValue - minValue;

    regenerate = true;
    postInvalidate();
}
```

Finally, we need to update the `getDataPoint()` method to allow us to get data from different data sets:

```
private float getDataPoint(int i, int index) {
    float data = (dataPoints[index].get(i) - minValue) / verticalDelta;
    return invertVerticalAxis ? 1.f - data : data;
}
```

With all these methods, we can update our path generation code to generate multiple Paths. If the data set for that graph is not defined, it'll not generate the Path.

```
for (int j = 0; j < 2; j++) {
    if (dataPoints[j] != null) {
        float x = leftPadding;
        float y = height * getDataPoint(0, j) + topPadding;

        graphPath[j].moveTo(x, y);
        circlePath[j].addCircle(x, y, 10, Path.Direction.CW);

        for (int i = 1; i < dataPoints[j].size(); i++) {
            x = width * (((float) i + 1) / dataPoints[j].size()) +
            leftPadding;
            y = height * getDataPoint(i, j) + topPadding;

            graphPath[j].lineTo(x, y);
            circlePath[j].addCircle(x, y, 10, Path.Direction.CW);
        }
    }
}
```

The rendering code, which is just iterating through all the generated Paths and drawing them with their correspondent Paint objects:

```
for (int j = 0; j < graphPath.length; j++) {
    canvas.drawPath(graphPath[j], linePaint[j]);
    canvas.drawPath(circlePath[j], circlePaint[j]);
}
```

If we run this example with two sets of random data, we'll see something similar to the following screen:

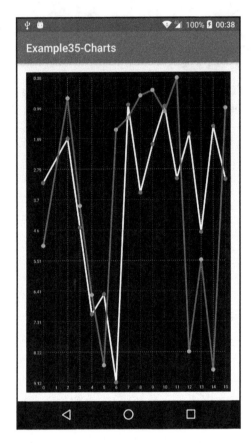

Zooming and scrolling

Another interesting feature we can implement into our custom view is the ability to zoom and scroll. Like we did in our previous chapter, we'll use the `ScaleDetector` class from Android to detect the pinch gesture and update the zoom in our custom view.

Implementation will be quite different from the previous chapter. In this case, we'll do it in a simpler way. As we want to zoom everything, we'll just apply a `canvas` transformation instead of regenerating the scaled `Path` objects again, but first, let's implement the gesture detector and add the ability to scroll and animate properties.

We can almost copy the same methods we used in our previous custom EPG View for animating variable logic and checking if we still have an unfinished animation:

```
private boolean missingAnimations() {
    if (Math.abs(scrollXTarget - scrollX) > ANIM_THRESHOLD)
        return true;

    if (Math.abs(scrollYTarget - scrollY) > ANIM_THRESHOLD)
        return true;

    return false;
}

private void animateLogic() {
    long currentTime = SystemClock.elapsedRealtime();
    accTime += currentTime - timeStart;
    timeStart = currentTime;

    while (accTime > TIME_THRESHOLD) {
        scrollX += (scrollXTarget - scrollX) / 4.f;
        scrollY += (scrollYTarget - scrollY) / 4.f;
        accTime -= TIME_THRESHOLD;
    }

    float factor = ((float) accTime) / TIME_THRESHOLD;
    float nextScrollX = scrollX + (scrollXTarget - scrollX) / 4.f;
    float nextScrollY = scrollY + (scrollYTarget - scrollY) / 4.f;

    frScrollX = scrollX * (1.f - factor) + nextScrollX * factor;
    frScrollY = scrollY * (1.f - factor) + nextScrollY * factor;
}
```

We can also add, almost as it is, the code for checking drag events, sending the touch events to the scale detector and scroll the screen depending on the drag amount:

```
@Override
public boolean onTouchEvent(MotionEvent event) {
    scaleDetector.onTouchEvent(event);

    if (zooming) {
        invalidate();
        zooming = false;
        return true;
    }

    switch(event.getAction()) {
        case MotionEvent.ACTION_DOWN:
```

```
                    dragX = event.getX();
                    dragY = event.getY();

                    getParent().requestDisallowInterceptTouchEvent(true);
                    dragged = false;
                    return true;

            case MotionEvent.ACTION_UP:
                    getParent().requestDisallowInterceptTouchEvent(false);
                    return true;

            case MotionEvent.ACTION_MOVE:
                    float newX = event.getX();
                    float newY = event.getY();

                    scrollScreen(dragX - newX, dragY - newY);

                    dragX = newX;
                    dragY = newY;
                    dragged = true;
                    return true;
            default:
                    return false;
        }
    }

    private void scrollScreen(float dx, float dy) {
        scrollXTarget += dx;
        scrollYTarget += dy;

        if (scrollXTarget < 0) scrollXTarget = 0;
        if (scrollYTarget < 0) scrollYTarget = 0;

        if (scrollXTarget > getWidth() * scale - getWidth()) {
            scrollXTarget = getWidth() * scale - getWidth();
        }

        if (scrollYTarget > getHeight() * scale - getHeight()) {
            scrollYTarget = getHeight() * scale - getHeight();
        }

        invalidate();
    }
```

We've defined a variable named scale that will control the amount of zooming, or scaling, we're doing to our graph custom view. Let's now write the implementation of the `scaleDetector`:

```
scaleDetector = new ScaleGestureDetector(context, new
ScaleGestureDetector.SimpleOnScaleGestureListener() {
    private float focusX;
    private float focusY;
    private float scrollCorrectionX = 0.f;
    private float scrollCorrectionY = 0.f;

    @Override
    public boolean onScaleBegin(ScaleGestureDetector detector) {
        zooming = true;
        focusX = detector.getFocusX();
        focusY = detector.getFocusY();
        scrollCorrectionX = focusX * scale - scrollXTarget;
        scrollCorrectionY = focusY * scale - scrollYTarget;
        return true;
    }

    public boolean onScale(ScaleGestureDetector detector) {
        scale *= detector.getScaleFactor();
        scale = Math.max(1.f, Math.min(scale, 2.f));

        float currentX = focusX * scale - scrollXTarget;
        float currentY = focusY * scale - scrollYTarget;

        scrollXTarget += currentX - scrollCorrectionX;
        scrollYTarget += currentY - scrollCorrectionY;

        invalidate();
        return true;
    }

    @Override
    public void onScaleEnd(ScaleGestureDetector detector) {
        zooming = true;
    }
});
```

We also implemented a scroll correction mechanism to keep where we're zooming as centered as possible. In this case, we had to implement it on both the horizontal and the vertical axis. The main idea behind the algorithm is to calculate the horizontal and vertical position of the focused point of the gesture and when changing the zoom, adjusting the scroll position to keep it at the same place.

Now, our `onDraw()` method will simply start with the following:

```
animateLogic();

canvas.save();

canvas.translate(-frScrollX, -frScrollY);
canvas.scale(scale, scale);
```

We need to check and process the animation cycles by calling `animateLogic()`, then let's behave properly and save our `canvas` state, apply a translation by the scrolling values `frScrollX` and `frScrollY`, and scale the whole `canvas` by the `scale` variable.

Everything we'll render will be displaced by the scroll position and scaled by the value of the scale variable. Before finishing the method, we've to restore our `canvas` and trigger a new redraw cycle if not all the property animations have finished:

```
canvas.restore();
if (missingAnimations()) invalidate();
```

See the full example source code in the `Example35-Charts` folder on the GitHub repository.

Summary

In this chapter we have seen how to build a charts custom view to draw graphs in our Android applications. We have also quickly covered how to manage paddings, RTL / LTR support, and we have finally added some complexity to our custom view by supporting multiple data sets or adding the features of zooming and scrolling.

Also, the way we've implemented this custom view; using independent data ranges and adapting it dynamically to the screen, means it'll automatically adjust to any screen resolution or for example, to an orientation change. This is usually a good practice and will prevent many issues when testing our custom view on several devices. In addition, making the sizes of everything we draw on the screen depend on the screen density, like we did in our previous example, will make the portability even easier.

In the next chapter, we will show how to build a custom view using the 3D rendering capabilities we've introduced in previous chapters.

11
Creating a 3D Spinning Wheel Menu

With the exception of `Chapter 5`, *Introducing 3D Custom Views*, where we explained how to build custom views using OpenGL ES, all the other examples in this book use the 2D drawing methods available from the `Canvas` class. In the last two chapters, we have seen how to build slightly more complex custom views, but none of them were using any 3D rendering techniques. So, in this chapter, we will show how to build and customize a full custom 3D view and how to interact with it.

With more detail, we will cover the following in this chapter:

- Adding interactions to a 3D custom view
- Adding a `GestureDetector` to manage complex gestures
- Using a `scroller` to manage scroll and fling gestures
- Rendering text into textures and drawing them on OpenGL ES
- Generating geometry programmatically

Creating an interactive 3D custom view

In `Chapter 5`, *Introducing 3D Custom Views*, we saw how to create a very simple rotating cube using OpenGL ES. Starting from that example and by just adding a way to react to user interactions, we can create the foundations of a more complex and interactive custom view.

Adding interactions

Let's start by using the code from the `Example25-GLDrawing`. Processing user interactions is quite simple, as we have already seen in our previous examples. We don't have to do anything different than before, just override the `onTouchEvent()` method in our class extending `GLSurfaceView` and react properly to the different MotionEvents we will receive. For instance, if we don't return `true` when we receive a `MotionEvent.ACTION_DOWN`, we will not receive any further events, as we are basically saying that we are not handling the event.

Once we have the source code of the example, let's add a simple implementation of the `onTouchEvent()` that tracks drag events:

```java
private float dragX;
private float dragY;

@Override
public boolean onTouchEvent(MotionEvent event) {
    switch(event.getAction()) {
        case MotionEvent.ACTION_DOWN:
            dragX = event.getX();
            dragY = event.getY();

            getParent().requestDisallowInterceptTouchEvent(true);
            return true;

        case MotionEvent.ACTION_UP:
            getParent().requestDisallowInterceptTouchEvent(false);
            return true;

        case MotionEvent.ACTION_MOVE:
            float newX = event.getX();
            float newY = event.getY();

            angleTarget -= (dragX - newX) / 3.f;

            dragX = newX;
            dragY = newY;
            return true;
        default:
            return false;
    }
}
```

We'll use the drag amount to change the angle of rotation of the cube, as we will see in the following code snippets. In addition, later in this chapter, we will see how we can do this animation using a `scroller` class, but, for the moment, let's use a fixed time-step mechanism:

```
private float angle = 0.f;
private float angleTarget = 0.f;
private float angleFr = 0.f;

private void animateLogic() {
    long currentTime = SystemClock.elapsedRealtime();
    accTime += currentTime - timeStart;
    timeStart = currentTime;

    while (accTime > TIME_THRESHOLD) {
        angle += (angleTarget - angle) / 4.f;
        accTime -= TIME_THRESHOLD;
    }

    float factor = ((float) accTime) / TIME_THRESHOLD;
    float nextAngle = angle + (angleTarget - angle) / 4.f;

    angleFr = angle * (1.f - factor) + nextAngle * factor;
}
```

It uses the same principles as what we have been doing in previous examples, execute a single tick of logic every `TIME_THRESHOLD` milliseconds. The cube angle value will be interpolated between the current state and the next state depending on the time remaining to the execution of the next logic tick. This interpolated value will be stored on the `angleFr` variable.

We have also done some changes to the `onSurfaceChanged` to use the perspective projection mode instead of using `Matrix.frustrumM`. The latter defines the six clipping planes: near, far, top, bottom, left, and right. However, using `Matrix.perspective` allows us to define the projection matrix in terms of the camera field of view angle and two clipping planes: near and far. It might be handier in some situations, but at the end of the day, both methods achieve the same objective:

```
@Override
public void onSurfaceChanged(GL10 unused, int width, int height) {
    GLES20.glViewport(0, 0, width, height);

    float ratio = (float) width / height;
    Matrix.perspectiveM(mProjectionMatrix, 0, 90, ratio, 0.1f, 7.f);
}
```

Finally, we have got to do some changes to the `onDrawFrame()` method:

```
@Override
public void onDrawFrame(GL10 unused) {
animateLogic();
    GLES20.glClearColor(1.0f, 0.0f, 0.0f, 1.0f);
    GLES20.glClear(GLES20.GL_COLOR_BUFFER_BIT |
GLES20.GL_DEPTH_BUFFER_BIT);

    Matrix.setLookAtM(mViewMatrix, 0,
            0, 0, -3,
            0f, 0f, 0f,
            0f, 1.0f, 0.0f);

    Matrix.multiplyMM(mMVPMatrix, 0, mProjectionMatrix, 0, mViewMatrix, 0);
    Matrix.rotateM(mMVPMatrix, 0, angleFr, 0.f, 1.f, 0.f);
    Matrix.rotateM(mMVPMatrix, 0, 5.f, 1.f, 0.f, 0.f);
    GLES20.glUseProgram(shaderProgram);
    int positionHandle = GLES20.glGetAttribLocation(shaderProgram,
"vPosition");
    GLES20.glVertexAttribPointer(positionHandle, 3,
            GLES20.GL_FLOAT, false,
            0, vertexBuffer);

    int texCoordHandle = GLES20.glGetAttribLocation(shaderProgram, "aTex");
    GLES20.glVertexAttribPointer(texCoordHandle, 2, GLES20.GL_FLOAT, false,
                        0, texBuffer);
    int mMVPMatrixHandle = GLES20.glGetUniformLocation(shaderProgram,
                        "uMVPMatrix");

    GLES20.glUniformMatrix4fv(mMVPMatrixHandle, 1, false, mMVPMatrix, 0);

    int texHandle = GLES20.glGetUniformLocation(shaderProgram, "sTex");
    GLES20.glActiveTexture(GLES20.GL_TEXTURE0);
    GLES20.glBindTexture(GLES20.GL_TEXTURE_2D, textureId);
    GLES20.glUniform1i(texHandle, 0);

    GLES20.glEnable(GLES20.GL_DEPTH_TEST);
    GLES20.glEnableVertexAttribArray(texHandle);
    GLES20.glEnableVertexAttribArray(positionHandle);
    GLES20.glDrawElements(
            GLES20.GL_TRIANGLES, index.length,
            GLES20.GL_UNSIGNED_SHORT, indexBuffer);

    GLES20.glDisableVertexAttribArray(positionHandle);
    GLES20.glDisableVertexAttribArray(texHandle);
    GLES20.glDisable(GLES20.GL_DEPTH_TEST);
}
```

Basically, the changes we have got to make are to call the `animateLogic()` method to execute any pending logic tick and use the interpolated `angleFr` variable for the rotation angle. If we run this example, we will get the same cube we had in `Example25` but, in this case, we can control the animation by dragging horizontally on the screen. We have also got to remember, that there is no need to call `invalidate` or `postInvalidate` as when extending our class from `GLSurfaceView` and, unless specifically indicated, the screen will be constantly redrawn.

Improving interactions and animations

We have been using a fixed time-step mechanism to manage the animations, but let's see what advantages it gives us to use a `scroller` class provided by Android to handle the animations, instead of handling all the animations by ourselves.

First, let's create a `GestureDetector` instance to handle the touch events:

```
private GestureDetectorCompat gestureDetector =
        new GestureDetectorCompat(context, new MenuGestureListener());
```

We are using the `GestureDetectorCompat` from the support library to guarantee the same behavior on older versions of Android.

As we covered in `Chapter 3`, *Handling Events,* by introducing a `GestureDetector` we can greatly simplify our `onTouchEvent()`, as all the logic will be handled by the `MenuGestureListener` callback instead of being on the `onTouchEvent()`:

```
@Override
public boolean onTouchEvent(MotionEvent event) {
    return gestureDetector.onTouchEvent(event);
}
```

The `gestureDetector` requires an implementation of an `OnGestureListener`, but if we only want to implement some methods and not have to worry about the other methods exposed by the interface, we could just extend from `GestureDetector.SimpleOnGestureListener` and only override the methods we need. The `GestureDetector.SimpleOnGestureListener` class comes with a dummy empty implementation for all the methods exposed in the `OnGestureListener` interface.

`SimpleOnGestureListener` also implements other interfaces to make our lives as software engineers easier, but please refer to the Android documentation for more information.

Let's then create our own internal class, MenuGestureListener, extending from
GestureDetector.SimpleOnGestureListener:

```
class MenuGestureListener extends
        GestureDetector.SimpleOnGestureListener {
    @Override
    public boolean onDown(MotionEvent e) {
        scroller.forceFinished(true);
        return true;
    }

    @Override
    public boolean onScroll(MotionEvent e1, MotionEvent e2, float
    distanceX,
    float distanceY) {
        scroller.computeScrollOffset();
        int lastX = scroller.getCurrX();

        scroller.forceFinished(true);
        scroller.startScroll(lastX, 0, -(int) (distanceX + 0.5f), 0);
        return true;
    }

    @Override
    public boolean onFling(MotionEvent e1, MotionEvent e2, float
    velocityX, float velocityY) {
        scroller.computeScrollOffset();
        int lastX = scroller.getCurrX();

        scroller.forceFinished(true);
        scroller.fling(lastX,
                0,
                (int) (velocityX/4.f),
                0,
                -360*100,
                360*100,
                0,
                0);
        return true;
    }
}
```

As we have mentioned before, even if it's an OnGestureListener implementation, we
have got to return true on the onDown() method. Otherwise, the onScroll() or
onFling() methods from our OnGestureListener implementation won't be called
whenever there is a scroll or fling event.

Anyway, we still have some work to do on the `onDown()` method: We have got to stop any running animation so the custom view will feel more reactive to the user.

We have implemented two other methods: `onScroll()` and `onFling()`. They're both managing different gestures that directly map to different ways of scrolling. Whenever we are dragging on the screen, the `onScroll()` method will be called as we will be actually scrolling. On the other hand, when we do a fling gesture; that is, when the user drags and lifts the finger from the screen very quickly, we need to take into consideration other parameters, such as the velocity and friction of the animation. When the gesture finishes, the animation will still run for some time, slowing down until stopping depending on the defined friction. In that case, the `onFling()` method from our listener will be called with the horizontal and vertical velocity of the fling event, leaving the friction to be handled by us.

In both events, we will be using a `scroller` class to simplify the calculations. We could do it ourselves but, although implementing the `onScroll()` logic would be quite straightforward, implementing the `onFling()` animation properly would require some calculations and complexities that we can take for granted by using a `scroller` class.

On the `onScroll()` implementation, we are simply calling the `startScroll` method of the `scroller` from the current position and the dragged distance. To get the current position, we have got to call `scroller.computeScrollOffset` first. If we don't call it, the current value will always be zero. Once we have called this method, we can retrieve the current value of the `scroller` by using the `getCurrX` method.

As in our listener we are getting the distance as a floating point and `startScroll` only accepts integer values, we will round the `distanceX` value by just adding 0.5 and then converting it in to an integer value.

Similarly, on the `onFling()` implementation we will be calling the `fling` method of the `scroller`. We'll get the current position, as we have described in the `onScroll()` implementation, and we will adjust the velocity as it was too high from the point of view of animating a rotating cube. We have set the maximum and minimum values to 100 full turns of the cube as, in normal circumstances, we don't want to limit the rotation.

Now, by using a `scroller`, we can get rid of the `animateLogic()` method and all associated variables, as we will no longer need them. On both gestures, scroll and fling, the animations will be performed on the background and we can directly query the current animated value directly from the `scroller` instance.

The only changes we have got to do on the `onDraw()` method is to call the
`scroller.computeScrollOffset` method to have an updated value and, instead of using
the `angleFr` variable, get the value from the `scroller`:

```
Matrix.rotateM(mMVPMatrix, 0, scroller.getCurrX(), 0.f, 1.f, 0.f);
```

Adding actionable callbacks

Let's convert this into an actionable menu. We could map an action to each face of the cube.
As we are rotating the cube horizontally, or on the y axis, we could map an action to each of
the four available faces.

For added clarity, as currently the rotation might end in the middle of a face, let's add a
small feature: whenever the animation finishes, let's snap it to the closest face, so we'll
always have a fully aligned front face of the cube when there is no animation running.

Implementing snapping is fairly simple. We have got to check if the animation has finished
and, in that case, check which face is facing to the camera. We could do so by simply
dividing the current rotation angle by 90; 360 degrees split by four faces is 90 degrees each.
To see if we are closer to that face than from the next one, we have got to get the fractional
part of the rotation angle. If we calculate the angle modulo 90, we will get a number
between 0 and 89. If that result is smaller than half the degrees needed to switch from one
face to another, we will be on the right face. However, in the opposite case, if that result is
bigger than 45, or smaller than -45, we'd have to rotate to the next or previous face,
respectively. Let's write this small logic in our `onDraw()` method, just after the call to
`scroller.computeScrollOffset`:

```
if (scroller.isFinished()) {
    int lastX = scroller.getCurrX();
    int modulo = lastX % 90;
    int snapX = (lastX / 90) * 90;
    if (modulo >= 45) snapX += 90;
    if (modulo <- 45) snapX -= 90;

    if (lastX != snapX) {
        scroller.startScroll(lastX, 0, snapX - lastX, 0);
    }
}
```

To calculate the snap angle, we do an integer division by 90 and multiply the result by 90. As it's an integer division, it'll get rid of the decimal part and calculate the absolute angle value of that face. Another way of writing that code would be the following:

```
int face = lastX / 90;
int snapX = face * 90;
```

Then, depending on the modulo result, we are adding 90 or subtracting 90 to effectively go to the next or previous face.

Now, let's add the code to manage the user clicks. First, let's create an interface of a listener to delegate the handling of the event to that listener:

```
interface OnMenuClickedListener {
    void menuClicked(int option);
}
```

Also, let's add an `OnMenuClickedListener` variable to our class and a setter method:

```
private OnMenuClickedListener listener;

public void setOnMenuClickedListener(OnMenuClickedListener listener) {
    this.listener = listener;
}
```

Now, we can implement the `onSingleTapUp` method on the `MenuGestureListener`:

```
@Override
public boolean onSingleTapUp(MotionEvent e) {
    scroller.computeScrollOffset();
    int angle = scroller.getCurrX();
    int face = (angle / 90) % 4;
    if (face < 0) face += 4;

    if (listener != null) listener.menuClicked(face);
    return true;
}
```

Let's also add an `id` to our custom view in the `activity_main` layout file, so we can get the `GLDrawer` view from the code:

```
<?xml version="1.0" encoding="utf-8"?>
<LinearLayout
    xmlns:android="http://schemas.android.com/apk/res/android"
    xmlns:tools="http://schemas.android.com/tools"
    android:id="@+id/activity_main"
    android:layout_width="match_parent"
    android:layout_height="match_parent"
```

```
            android:orientation="vertical"
            android:padding="@dimen/activity_vertical_margin"
            tools:context="com.packt.rrafols.draw.MainActivity">

    <com.packt.rrafols.draw.GLDrawer
    android:id="@+id/gldrawer"
            android:layout_width="match_parent"
            android:layout_height="match_parent"/>
    </LinearLayout>
```

Finally, modify the `MainActivity` class to create an `OnMenuClickedListener` and set it to the `GLDrawer` view:

```
@Override
protected void onCreate(Bundle savedInstanceState) {
    super.onCreate(savedInstanceState);
    setContentView(R.layout.activity_main);
    GLDrawer glDrawer = (GLDrawer) findViewById(R.id.gldrawer);
    glDrawer.setOnMenuClickedListener(new
    GLDrawer.OnMenuClickedListener() {
        @Override
        public void menuClicked(int option) {
            Log.i("Example36-Menu3D", "option clicked " + option);
        }
    });
}
```

If we run this example, we will see how the `MainActivity` is logging which face are we clicking on the cube:

```
com.packt.rrafols.draw I/Example36-Menu3D: option clicked 3
com.packt.rrafols.draw I/Example36-Menu3D: option clicked 2.
```

We will also see how the snapping works. Play with it to see how it snaps to the current face, to the next one, or to the previous one if we are scrolling backwards.

Customizations

We are still rendering the cube the same way we left it in `Example25`. Let's change it to draw every cube face in a different solid color. We can define a different color per vertex, but as vertices are shared between faces, their colors will be interpolated.

```
colorBuffer.put(colors);
colorBuffer.position(0);
```

Update the pixel and vertex Shaders:

```
private final String vertexShaderCode =
        "uniform mat4 uMVPMatrix;" +
        "attribute vec4 vPosition;" +
        "attribute vec4 aColor;" +
        "varying vec4 vColor;" +
        "void main() {" +
        "  gl_Position = uMVPMatrix * vPosition;" +
        "  vColor = aColor;" +
        "}";

private final String fragmentShaderCode =
        "precision mediump float;" +
        "varying vec4 vColor;" +
        "void main() {" +
        "  gl_FragColor = vColor;" +
        "}";
```

To make it more configurable, let's create a public setColors() method on GLDrawer to change the colors:

```
public void setColors(int[] faceColors) {
    glRenderer.setColors(faceColors);
}
```

The implementation on the Renderer is as follows:

```
private void setColors(int[] faceColors) {
    colors = new float[4 * 4 * faceColors.length];
    int wOffset = 0;
    for (int faceColor : faceColors) {
        float[] color = hexToRGBA(faceColor);
        for(int j = 0; j < 4; j++) {
            colors[wOffset++] = color[0];
            colors[wOffset++] = color[1];
            colors[wOffset++] = color[2];
            colors[wOffset++] - color[3];
        }
    }
    ByteBuffer cbb = ByteBuffer.allocateDirect(colors.length *
    (Float.SIZE /8));
    cbb.order(ByteOrder.nativeOrder());

    colorBuffer = cbb.asFloatBuffer();
```

```
        colorBuffer.put(colors);
        colorBuffer.position(0);
    }
```

For simplicity, we will pass the colors as an integer, instead of a float array, so we can use colors in hexadecimal encoding, for example. To convert an integer color to a float array we can use a simple helper method:

```
private float[] hexToRGBA(int color) {
    float[] out = new float[4];

    int a = (color >> 24) & 0xff;
    int r = (color >> 16) & 0xff;
    int g = (color >>  8) & 0xff;
    int b = (color      ) & 0xff;

    out[0] = ((float) r) / 255.f;
    out[1] = ((float) g) / 255.f;
    out[2] = ((float) b) / 255.f;
    out[3] = ((float) a) / 255.f;
    return out;
}
```

To update the example, let's set some colors using the method we have just added:

```
glDrawer.setColors(new int[] {
        0xff4a90e2,
        0xff161616,
        0xff594236,
        0xffff5964,
        0xff8aea92,
        0xfffe74c
});
```

If we run the example, we will get something like the following screenshot:

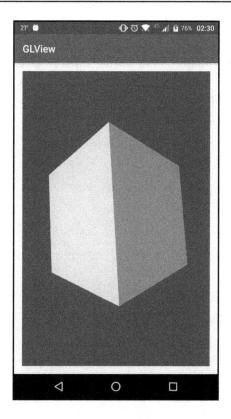

Check the full source code of this example in the Example36-Menu3D folder in the GitHub repository.

Beyond the basic implementation

We have got a very basic and actionable 3D menu but, in order for it to be used on a production application, we have got to add some more details. For instance, we can now select a different menu option depending on the face of the cube we are selecting, but unless we are doing a very simple color picker, we'd be selecting an option completely blind, as we won't know which face does exactly what.

One way to solve this is to render some text depending on which face is selected, but on OpenGL ES we can't simply just call drawText and render some text, like we are used to do when using a Canvas. Also, in this example, there are only four selectable faces or options; let's make some changes so we can have more selectable options.

Rendering text

As we have just mentioned, to render text, we can't just call a `drawText` method that will render some text in 3D inside our small 3D scene. Actually, we'd be using `drawText`, but just to render it on a background `Bitmap` that would be used as a texture for an additional plane we will be rendering.

In order to do so, we'd have to define the geometry of that plane:

```
private float planeCoords[] = {
        -1.f, -1.f, -1.4f,
        -1.f,  1.f, -1.4f,
         1.f,  1.f, -1.4f,
         1.f, -1.f, -1.4f,
};

private short[] planeIndex = {
        0, 1, 2,
        0, 2, 3
};

private float texCoords[] = {
        1.f, 1.f,
        1.f, 0.f,
        0.f, 0.f,
        0.f, 1.f
};
```

As the cube front face is at z-coordinate -1.f, this plane will be at -1.4f, so 0.4f in front of it, otherwise it might get occluded by the cube.

We have got to add the vertex and fragment `Shader` again, to render with a texture. Although we will not replace the current `Shader` we have got in our code, we will have to live with both sets of `Shader`:

```
private final String vertexShaderCodeText =
        "uniform mat4 uMVPMatrix;" +
        "attribute vec4 vPosition;" +
        "attribute vec2 aTex;" +
        "varying vec2 vTex;" +
        "void main() {" +
        "  gl_Position = uMVPMatrix * vPosition;" +
        "  vTex = aTex;" +
        "}";

private final String fragmentShaderCodeText =
        "precision mediump float;" +
```

```
"uniform sampler2D sTex;" +
"varying vec2 vTex;" +
"void main() {" +
"  gl_FragColor = texture2D(sTex, vTex);" +
"}";
```

Let's also update the initBuffers method to initialize both sets of Buffers:

```
private void initBuffers() {
    ByteBuffer vbb = ByteBuffer.allocateDirect(quadCoords.length
            * (Float.SIZE / 8));
    vbb.order(ByteOrder.nativeOrder());

    vertexBuffer = vbb.asFloatBuffer();
    vertexBuffer.put(quadCoords);
    vertexBuffer.position(0);

    ByteBuffer ibb = ByteBuffer.allocateDirect(index.length
            * (Short.SIZE / 8));
    ibb.order(ByteOrder.nativeOrder());

    indexBuffer = ibb.asShortBuffer();
    indexBuffer.put(index);
    indexBuffer.position(0);

    ByteBuffer cbb = ByteBuffer.allocateDirect(colors.length
            * (Float.SIZE / 8));
    cbb.order(ByteOrder.nativeOrder());

    colorBuffer = cbb.asFloatBuffer();
    colorBuffer.put(colors);
    colorBuffer.position(0);


    vbb = ByteBuffer.allocateDirect(planeCoords.length
            * (Float.SIZE / 8));
    vbb.order(ByteOrder.nativeOrder());

    vertexTextBuffer = vbb.asFloatBuffer();
    vertexTextBuffer.put(planeCoords);
    vertexTextBuffer.position(0);

    ibb = ByteBuffer.allocateDirect(planeIndex.length
            * (Short.SIZE / 8));
    ibb.order(ByteOrder.nativeOrder());

    indexTextBuffer = ibb.asShortBuffer();
    indexTextBuffer.put(planeIndex);
```

```
            indexTextBuffer.position(0);

            ByteBuffer tbb = ByteBuffer.allocateDirect(texCoords.length
                    * (Float.SIZE / 8));
            tbb.order(ByteOrder.nativeOrder());

            texBuffer = tbb.asFloatBuffer();
            texBuffer.put(texCoords);
            texBuffer.position(0);
        }
```

As we can see, this method is allocating both sets of Buffers: one set for the cube and another for the plane we will use to draw the text. We have got to do a similar approach for the vertex and fragment Shaders, we have got to load and link both sets of Shaders:

```
        private void initShaders() {
            int vertexShader = loadShader(GLES20.GL_VERTEX_SHADER,
        vertexShaderCode);
            int fragmentShader = loadShader(GLES20.GL_FRAGMENT_SHADER,
            fragmentShaderCode);

            shaderProgram = GLES20.glCreateProgram();
            GLES20.glAttachShader(shaderProgram, vertexShader);
            GLES20.glAttachShader(shaderProgram, fragmentShader);
            GLES20.glLinkProgram(shaderProgram);

            vertexShader = loadShader(GLES20.GL_VERTEX_SHADER,
        vertexShaderCodeText);
            fragmentShader = loadShader(GLES20.GL_FRAGMENT_SHADER,
            fragmentShaderCodeText);

            shaderTextProgram = GLES20.glCreateProgram();
            GLES20.glAttachShader(shaderTextProgram, vertexShader);
            GLES20.glAttachShader(shaderTextProgram, fragmentShader);
            GLES20.glLinkProgram(shaderTextProgram);
        }
```

We are attaching the shaders we will use to draw the text in a texture to another Shader program we will store in the shaderTextProgram variable. Depending on what we want to render we could now switch from shaderProgram or shaderTextProgram.

Let's now create a method that returns a Bitmap with a text centered on it:

```
        private Bitmap createBitmapFromText(String text) {
            Bitmap out = Bitmap.createBitmap(512, 512,
            Bitmap.Config.ARGB_8888);
            out.eraseColor(0x00000000);
```

```
Paint textPaint = new Paint();
textPaint.setAntiAlias(true);
textPaint.setColor(0xffffffff);
textPaint.setTextSize(60);
textPaint.setStrokeWidth(2.f);
textPaint.setStyle(Paint.Style.FILL);

Rect textBoundaries = new Rect();
textPaint.getTextBounds(text, 0, text.length(), textBoundaries);

Canvas canvas = new Canvas(out);
for (int i = 0; i < 2; i++) {
    canvas.drawText(text,
            (canvas.getWidth() - textBoundaries.width()) / 2.f,
            (canvas.getHeight() - textBoundaries.height()) / 2.f +
            textBoundaries.height(), textPaint);
    textPaint.setColor(0xff000000);
    textPaint.setStyle(Paint.Style.STROKE);
}
return out;
}
```

This method creates a `Bitmap` of 512 by 512 with eight bits per color component and four components: alpha, or transparency, red, green, and blue. Then, it is creating a `Paint` object with the color and size of the text, getting the text boundaries in order to center it on the `Bitmap` and drawing the text twice on the `Canvas` object we can get from the `Bitmap`. Text is drawn twice, because it first draws the text with a solid white color and then, as we change the `Paint` object style to `STROKE`, it's draws the silhouette using a black color.

The code we had in previous examples to load a texture was loading it from a local resource. As it was converting it into an unscaled `Bitmap`, we could reuse most of that code to load our generated `Bitmap`. Let's recover the `loadTexture()` method we already had, but let's change it to use a helper method to upload a `Bitmap` into a `Texture`:

```
private int loadTexture(int resId) {
    final int[] textureIds = new int[1];
    GLES20.glGenTextures(1, textureIds, 0);

    if (textureIds[0] == 0) return -1;

    // do not scale the bitmap depending on screen density
    final BitmapFactory.Options options = new BitmapFactory.Options();
    options.inScaled = false;

    final Bitmap textureBitmap =
    BitmapFactory.decodeResource(getResources(),
```

```
        resId, options);
        attachBitmapToTexture(textureIds[0], textureBitmap);

        return textureIds[0];
    }
```

The implementation of the helper method is as follows:

```
    private void attachBitmapToTexture(int textureId, Bitmap textureBitmap) {
        GLES20.glBindTexture(GLES20.GL_TEXTURE_2D, textureId);

        GLES20.glTexParameteri(GLES20.GL_TEXTURE_2D,
                GLES20.GL_TEXTURE_MIN_FILTER, GLES20.GL_LINEAR);

        GLES20.glTexParameteri(GLES20.GL_TEXTURE_2D,
                GLES20.GL_TEXTURE_MAG_FILTER, GLES20.GL_LINEAR);

        GLES20.glTexParameterf(GLES20.GL_TEXTURE_2D,
                GLES20.GL_TEXTURE_WRAP_S, GLES20.GL_CLAMP_TO_EDGE);

        GLES20.glTexParameterf(GLES20.GL_TEXTURE_2D,
                GLES20.GL_TEXTURE_WRAP_T, GLES20.GL_CLAMP_TO_EDGE);

        GLUtils.texImage2D(GLES20.GL_TEXTURE_2D, 0, textureBitmap, 0);
    }
```

We have only got to create a method that puts everything together: that is, one that generates a `Bitmap` from a text, generates a `textureIds`, uploads the `Bitmap` as a texture, and recycles the `Bitmap`:

```
    private int generateTextureFromText(String text) {
        final int[] textureIds = new int[1];
        GLES20.glGenTextures(1, textureIds, 0);

        Bitmap textureBitmap = createBitmapFromText(text);
        attachBitmapToTexture(textureIds[0], textureBitmap);
        textureBitmap.recycle();
        return textureIds[0];
    }
```

Using this method, we can now generate a different texture for each face of the cube:

```
    @Override
    public void onSurfaceCreated(GL10 unused, EGLConfig config) {
        initBuffers();
        initShaders();

        textureId = new int[4];
```

```
        for (int i = 0; i < textureId.length; i++) {
            textureId[i] = generateTextureFromText("Option " + (i + 1));
        }
    }
```

We can now add at the bottom of the `onDraw()` method some additional code to render a plane in front of each face of the cube:

```
GLES20.glUseProgram(shaderTextProgram);
positionHandle = GLES20.glGetAttribLocation(shaderTextProgram,
"vPosition");

GLES20.glVertexAttribPointer(positionHandle, 3,
        GLES20.GL_FLOAT, false,
        0, vertexTextBuffer);

int texCoordHandle = GLES20.glGetAttribLocation(shaderTextProgram, "aTex");
GLES20.glVertexAttribPointer(texCoordHandle, 2,
        GLES20.GL_FLOAT, false,
        0, texBuffer);

int texHandle = GLES20.glGetUniformLocation(shaderTextProgram, "sTex");
GLES20.glActiveTexture(GLES20.GL_TEXTURE0);
GLES20.glEnable(GLES20.GL_BLEND);
GLES20.glBlendFunc(GLES20.GL_SRC_ALPHA, GLES20.GL_ONE_MINUS_SRC_ALPHA);

for (int i = 0; i < 4; i++) {
    GLES20.glBindTexture(GLES20.GL_TEXTURE_2D, textureId[i]);
    GLES20.glUniform1i(texHandle, 0);

    mMVPMatrixHandle = GLES20.glGetUniformLocation(shaderTextProgram,
    "uMVPMatrix");
    GLES20.glUniformMatrix4fv(mMVPMatrixHandle, 1, false, mMVPMatrix,
    0);

    GLES20.glEnableVertexAttribArray(texHandle);
    GLES20.glEnableVertexAttribArray(positionHandle);
    GLES20.glDrawElements(
            GLES20.GL_TRIANGLES, planeIndex.length,
            GLES20.GL_UNSIGNED_SHORT, indexTextBuffer);

    GLES20.glDisableVertexAttribArray(positionHandle);
    GLES20.glDisableVertexAttribArray(texHandle);

    Matrix.rotateM(mMVPMatrix, 0, -90.f, 0.f, 1.f, 0.f);
}

GLES20.glDisable(GLES20.GL_BLEND);
```

```
GLES20.glDisable(GLES20.GL_DEPTH_TEST);
```

As we can see, we are changing the `positionHandle` to the plane geometry, enabling the texture vertex array and, in addition, we are enabling the blending mode. As the text texture will be transparent with the exception of the text, we need to enable blending or otherwise, OpenGL ES will render the transparent pixels as black.

To draw different planes, one for each horizontal face of the cube, we are doing a small loop where we bind a different texture and rotate by 90 degrees on each iteration.

If we run this example, we will see something similar to the following screenshot:

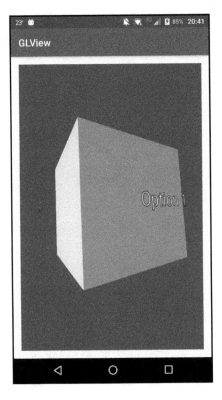

Multiple faces

Now that we have added the ability to render some text on top of the faces of the cube, we can know what we are selecting when clicking an option, but we are still limited to four different options. Currently, we have got the geometry hardcoded in the code in several arrays. If we want to make the number of options, or number or faces, dynamic we'd have to generate, programmatically, both the geometry and the face indexes.

Luckily for us, our starting point is to have several choices in a 3D circle, so we only have to generate a hollow cylinder with several faces, exactly as much as the number of options we'd like to have.

Let's add a method to the GLDrawer custom view class, allowing us to set the number of options and faces that we will have:

```
public void setNumOptions(int options) {
    double halfAngle = Math.PI / options;
    float[] coords = new float[options * 3 * 4];
    int offset = 0;
    for (int i = 0; i < options; i++) {
        float angle = (float) (i * 2.f * Math.PI / options
                - Math.PI / 2.f - halfAngle);

        float nextAngle = (float) ((i + 1) * 2.f * Math.PI / options
                - Math.PI / 2.f - halfAngle);

        float x0 = (float) Math.cos(angle) * 1.2f;
        float x1 = (float) Math.cos(nextAngle) * 1.2f;
        float z0 = (float) Math.sin(angle) * 1.2f;
        float z1 = (float) Math.sin(nextAngle) * 1.2f;

        coords[offset++] = x0;
        coords[offset++] = -1.f;
        coords[offset++] = z0;

        coords[offset++] = x1;
        coords[offset++] = -1.f;
        coords[offset++] = z1;

        coords[offset++] = x0;
        coords[offset++] = 1.f;
        coords[offset++] = z0;

        coords[offset++] = x1;
        coords[offset++] = 1.f;
        coords[offset++] = z1;
    }
```

```
        short[] index = new short[options * 6];
        for (int i = 0; i < options; i++) {
            index[i * 6 + 0] = (short) (i * 4 + 0);
            index[i * 6 + 1] = (short) (i * 4 + 1);
            index[i * 6 + 2] = (short) (i * 4 + 3);

            index[i * 6 + 3] = (short) (i * 4 + 0);
            index[i * 6 + 4] = (short) (i * 4 + 2);
            index[i * 6 + 5] = (short) (i * 4 + 3);
        }

        glRenderer.setCoordinates(options, coords, index);
    }
```

To generate diverse faces in a form of a cylinder is as easy as dividing the 360 degrees, or two times PI in radians, of a circle in the amount of faces we'd like to have. Here, we are dividing 2.f*Math.PI by the number of options and then multiplying it by the loop iterator. By calculating the sine and the cosine of that angle we can get two coordinates, usually x and y in a 2D projection, but in our specific case, we'd map it to x and z as we are setting the y coordinate to -1.f as the top vertical edge and 1.f as the bottom vertical edge. We are also calculating the next x and z coordinates, so we can create a face quad between these points.

We're generating four points for each face and we're indexing them as two triangles in the index array. This matches perfectly with the way we were generating colors before, as we're generating four color values for each face and now we are also generating exactly four vertices per face, each face will have a unique solid color.

At the end of the method, we're calling the setCoordinates() method of the GLRenderer, but that is very simple to implement:

```
    private void setCoordinates(int options, float[] coords, short[] index) {
        this.quadCoords = coords;
        this.index = index;
        this.options = options;
    }
```

This will work without touching anything else, as long as we call it before the surface is created. As we're talking about it, we have got to update the onSurfaceCreated() method to use the number of options we've set instead of the default four we had hardcoded in the code before:

```
    @Override
    public void onSurfaceCreated(GL10 unused, EGLConfig config) {
        initBuffers();
```

```
initShaders();

textureId = new int[options];
for (int i = 0; i < textureId.length; i++) {
    textureId[i] = generateTextureFromText("Option " + (i + 1));
}

faceAngle = 360.f / options;
}
```

We're also calculating the amount we've got to rotate to switch from one face to another. In our previous case it was easy, as there were four faces, 360 degrees divided by 4 is 90. Now, the calculation is still straightforward, but we've got to change the hardcoded 90 we had in the code by this new variable we've created, named faceAngle, the value of which is 360 divided by the number of options.

Let's test this new feature by calling it on the MainActivity, just after setting the different colors:

```
@Override
protected void onCreate(Bundle savedInstanceState) {
    super.onCreate(savedInstanceState);

    setContentView(R.layout.activity_main);

    GLDrawer glDrawer = (GLDrawer) findViewById(R.id.gldrawer);
    glDrawer.setOnMenuClickedListener(new
    GLDrawer.OnMenuClickedListener() {
        @Override
        public void menuClicked(int option) {
            Log.i("Example37-Menu3D", "option clicked " + option);
        }
    });
    glDrawer.setColors(new int[] {
            0xff4a90e2,
            0xff161616,
            0xff594236,
            0xffff5964,
            0xff8aea92,
            0xfffe74c
    });

    glDrawer.setNumOptions(6);
}
```

We've not specifically added a check, but the number of colors must be at least the same number of options or otherwise we will get an exception when rendering.

If we run this example, we will see something similar to the following screenshot, depending always on the current rotation:

Check out the full source code of this example in the Example37-Menu3D folder in the GitHub repository.

Summary

In this chapter, we've seen how to add interactions to a 3D custom view to make it interactive. In addition, we've seen how to use a `scroller` instance to manage both scroll and fling gestures and how to render text as a texture and use different geometry with different Buffers and different `Shaders`. At the end, we've also seen how we can easily generate geometry to make our custom view adaptable and dynamic.

In this book, we've seen how to build different kinds of custom views and to use both methods and classes from the Android SDK or to use our own, depending on our needs. We've also seen how to build both 2D and 3D custom views and to make them reactive to user input. At the end of the day, using all the APIs we've shown and a lot of creativity we can build any custom view we want. We still have to keep in mind that Android provides us with a great framework that is constantly evolving and contains plenty of good, and efficient, ways of drawing awesome UIs, but sometimes we want to build something special that we can't easily make using the standard APIs.

To learn even more about building Android UIs and custom views, there are plenty of tutorials on development blogs, several open sourced open views, and many sessions at meetups and conferences. Attending local meetups and conferences is a great way to not only learn about custom views, but also to stay up-to-date with Android development. There are many initiatives led by the Android community and I'd really like to encourage anyone to contribute in any way they can to keep the Android community alive and as awesome as it is.

Index